Infertile Ground

Surviving an Alcoholic Parent

Michael L Patton

Copyright © 2023 by Michael L Patton

All rights reserved.

First Edition

No part of this book may be reproduced in any form or by any electronic or mechanical means, including information storage and retrieval systems, without written permission from the author, except for the use of brief quotations in a book review.

For my Mother

Introduction

This is the tale of my childhood, my nuclear family with all that word implies, radioactive and toxic. Alcohol in significant quantities, when mixed with home and hearth can have devastating and unpredictable results on the bonds of family.

Imagine yourself as a child, lying in bed listening, straining to hear the dreaded sound of your father's car pulling into the drive while praying it never comes. Cringing when you hear his drunken footfalls in the hallway. Hoping he passes out before trouble begins.

I am the last surviving member of my family. Once I am gone, these moments of horror and acts of bravery, the physical and verbal assaults evaporate as if they never happened. The last wisp of smoke from a candle's dying flame. The damage done will be lost. Though he's gone some thirty-five years, his degradation and insults hurled remained and took root in the psyche of my siblings and myself as self-doubt and a diminished sense of worth. I believe those seeds sprouted and grew into cancer that claimed all three, two sisters and a brother. I have fought hard my entire life to be infertile ground, but I know the seeds lie dormant, waiting.

Fair Warning

My father would say I tell this story for attention. I don't think so. I tell it to exorcise it. After consideration, I wish to not carry this burden anymore. That's why I'm documenting all that happened here so I can leave it. Maybe it will teach somebody something if they read my story, or even a piece of it. I warn you. There are some sad parts. That's bound to happen with any story of consequence. I'm not looking for sympathy. That's not my goal. I'm simply recording what happened. The burden is not yours to take. My father should be the one shouldering the load. He should feel the weight and heft of it bearing down on him all the days of eternity. But he's the least likely to own up to any of the damage he caused. As I said, I'm writing this to be rid of the devastation. I'm sure it is of little use to others except perhaps to learn how not to be like my father or the pointlessness of shouldering such a load thrust upon you.

I'll let you judge whether I'm just seeking attention. I'd ask you to hold off until you've heard a fair piece of my story to help you understand.

Accusation of attention seeking is what my father threw at me my entire life. If I was feeling bad when I woke up with a sore throat or felt sick to my stomach and went to my mother to tell her I didn't feel like attending school, this would be my father's response.

"Aw, there ain't nothing wrong with him. Mike is just looking for attention." Those would be the first words out of my father's mouth.

It wouldn't matter if I had a rare virus or a splinter in my finger, his response was always the same. Someone had to be in the wrong if my father wasn't the room's primary focus. Being the youngest of the four children in the house, I was often the squeaky wheel since the others had learned this lesson.

I can remember only once when he showed concern for my well-being, which turned into a near-disaster. I was eight years old, and we were raking leaves in the yard. It was just my mom, my father, and me. They were on one side of a backyard metal shed, and I was on

Introduction

the other. It was a rare event when my father helped around the place, so he must have been sober for a change. I was standing on a pile of boards and old fencing, raking leaves from behind it when I felt a sudden sharp pain in my ankle like someone stuck a hot needle in me. When I looked down, I saw a black spider with an orange spot biting through my sweat sock. It jumped off before I could swat it, scrambling back into the woodpile. I grabbed my burning, throbbing ankle and moaned, "Mom, a spider bit me."

From the other side of the shed, I heard her say, "Well, bite it back."

She probably thought I was joking. My hand clamped around the outside of my sock. I must have moaned again because soon, my parents came running to help. When I described the spider, my father swept me in his arms (the only time I remember him doing that) and carried me into the trailer, our home. He laid me on the couch and ran into the bathroom as my mom called the doctor. My father returned and told me to turn my head. I remember wondering what he was going to do. After a few seconds, I felt more pain. When I looked back, he was slicing the bite with a razor blade. I assume he was trying to make it bleed out the poison as they did with snake bites in John Wayne movies. However, the razor was so thin that the cuts closed back without blood or poison draining. After several slashes to my throbbing ankle, I managed to yank my leg out of his grip. I grabbed it and started crying as he picked me up again and carried me to the car. We all piled into the front seat, me between my mom and dad. I remember speeding through town with the flashers pulsing and my dad honking at cars. We finally reached the doctor's office, and he carried me inside.

The doctor decided it was a male Black Widow based on my description of the size and color, assuring us it wasn't as poisonous as the female. He gave me the anti-venom and examined the bite. "What are all these little cuts here?" he asked.

My dad told him about the razor.

"All that accomplished was to upset him, so the poison moved faster toward his heart."

The doctor instructed my parents to keep me home from school the next day and that the ankle may be sore. When my dad came home from work the next evening, he never asked how I felt. Later that evening, I moved swiftly to the table after hearing my mom would let me have some ice cream.

"There ain't nothing wrong with that boy's ankle. He'd better go to school tomorrow," he declared showing how his concern was short-lived.

Such incidents, and those following, show why my father and I were never close. I avoided him when possible. He seemed to like my brother, teaching him to do welding and repairing. Of course, my brother tolerated him more than I could. My brother would go places and spend time with him when he was younger. As we got older, my brother's patience also grew shorter. Remember my warning before I get too far ahead of myself. Do not pick up this burden, not out of sympathy or guilt. Learn to be infertile ground for sad stories. They're only suitable for what you might learn from them, but leave them where you found them. They're at the side of the road for a reason.

Part One

Infancy

Chapter 1

Earliest Memories

There is no yardstick for measuring the depth of the scars when your beatings begin as a baby. They start at the skin, continue through bone and muscle, past your mind, and end deep into a child's soul.

I've thought about this. And I've spent years wondering when a father looked at his child and decided he hated it. What could that poor infant have possibly done to him?

To be honest, I'm not sure if I remember the first time my father hit me or if I am simply picturing it from when my mom told me the story through the years. I was on my mom's lap in the bedroom of what she would later call a shack on the banks of the Big Coal River in West Virginia. It wasn't exactly a shack because it had four rooms; a small living room, kitchen, my parent's bedroom, and a kids' bedroom. Driving by on the only road through town, you would most likely miss it because the roof was the same height as the road grade. It sat below the road on the bank of the river. A front porch with a swing and a back porch led to the washroom, where Mom had an old-fashioned washing machine with a ringer. My dad also installed an indoor toilet in the washroom, so we didn't have to use the outhouse.

My parents argued, which caused me to start cry, and my frustrated father hit me in the head, telling me to shut up. I am unsure if he used an open hand or a closed one, but you can imagine how well it worked to convince me to be quiet. I screamed even louder, as did my mom, who was now angrier than ever. Thus began my relationship with my father. It was early 1957 as I was lying on the bedspread, my mother examining my small head, which showed red, splotchy skin through the cotton-white hair sprinkling my scalp. She continued screaming obscenities at my father as he paced in and out of the room, angry at her, me, and himself.

I was the youngest of four children. My oldest sister, Rita who we called Ritzie, was twelve years older than me. She was born while my father nearly froze to death in World War II in France. Two days before the battle of the bulge began, he got word of her birth while in a foxhole in France. Annie or Annette, my youngest sister, was four years older, and my brother, Ernest Jr. who we called Buddy, was two years ahead of me.

I can't remember how that episode ended. It's lost in the noise that falls below the trauma level of a baby growing up in an alcoholic home. I imagine my mom stepped in to bear any further abuse.

I remember most of the stories of living in West Virginia from being told by my older siblings and mother. One of my mother's favorites to tell was when I went looking for our dog at the time. The story goes that my father was trying to do something, and being a curious young puppy, the dog got tangled up in his feet, causing my father to kick at it and yell, "get out of the way, you son-of-a-bitch." From that point on, that became the dog's name. My mother laughed as she described me standing by the road, looking for the dog, yelling "Here, Somabitch. Here, Somabitch," as a three-year-old.

There was a porch swing on the front porch, and we would all pile on it and sing "The Battle of New Orleans." It was a song that was popular at the time (1959) when Johnny Horton put out his version. It was a simple and poor existence for our family of six. With so many mouths to feed, my father was motivated to seek work out of state. So, around 1960 we moved to Delaware, where there was more demand for welders.

Because my father swore that living in the northeast was temporary, he purchased a mobile home for us and kept the house in West Virginia. It was typical of its day, fifty feet long and ten feet wide, with just two bedrooms. The living room was in the front, then the kitchen/dining room. The kids' bedroom was eight feet by ten, just long enough for a double bed, with a single bunk bed above it. The hallway ran through the middle of the room, with a closet and built-in drawers on the opposite wall. Behind that was the bathroom and then my parents' room. It was tight quarters with four kids, and privacy was non-existent. One benefit of living in a mobile home was that whenever my father inevitably created some kind of disturbance or scene, usually involving someone calling the police, it was easy to move somewhere else. Of course, this was no less traumatic for us kids, but at least we took our home with us when we were evicted. During this time, I became old enough to begin remembering things myself.

Chapter 2

What I Know About My Parents Early Years

Maybe I should slow down long enough to tell you what I know of my parents up to this point. The following I've pieced together through the years, and I will caution you that others told me this portion of the story, so take it as you see fit. The rest of my story is eye-witnessed.

My father, Ernest Arthur "Red" Patton was a middle child, if that means anything to you. He was the third child of seven, born in 1923. His father was a carpenter nicknamed "Shorty" because he was five-foot-two. When I knew him later in life, Grandpa Patton was a religious man, but I'm not sure if true when he was younger. I remember he had muscular forearms and was told by several of my uncles that he could drive a nail into a board with one blow from a hammer. I did hear him swear a few times when something he was working on did not cooperate, even after he was a deacon in the local Baptist church.

My father grew up during the Depression, which significantly impacted his family. His father was frequently absent in search of work to support the family. My father told me a story about being given an egg by someone at school. He told us this during one of his crying drunks, as my mom called them. It was raw and he decided to take the egg home to his mother so she could have it or use it. He put it carefully in his jacket pocket and protected it as best he could. On the school bus ride home, some kids were horsing around, and someone got shoved into my father, causing the egg to break. As I watched, this monster of a man cried like a baby, remembering how disappointed he was at being unable to give it to his mom. I guess he was a sensitive kid somewhere deep inside. It did bring home to me how hard the Depression was for his family.

I overheard my mom telling her sisters that my father had lived with a "grown-assed woman" when he was only thirteen. The way she said it implied it was a relationship, including sleeping with her. As a kid, when I heard it, it did nothing but confuse me. She seemed to think it was terrible, but I didn't understand until later. I wondered, at the time, if it had to do with saving money and food for his parents. Still, I never asked him about it since it seemed so secret, and given our relationship, I was sure it would probably earn me a slap or a punch in the mouth.

My mom, Marjorie Elouise "Marge" Droddy, was the oldest of five children. She was born in 1924 and was a year younger than my father. Her family didn't have it easy during the Depression. Her father worked in the oil fields, checking various wells in the hills of West Virginia, and I guess the work was a little steadier. She grew up in a home where she never heard he parents argue. She told me the one time they had words made quite an impression on her. Her father went to a local dance because he called square dances. The police arrested him for drinking after the dance. They called my grandmother, who bailed him out. When they returned home, her mother turned to her father and said flatly, "If you ever get arrested for being drunk again, don't call me to bail you out." That was the only "fight" my mother ever saw in her home.

She told of other times that her father would come home drinking and play drunk so that when the kids were helping him to bed, he would fall across one of them and trap them under his body. She told me about being worried about smothering until she could feel her father bounce as he chuckled, unable to hold it in. It was a pleasant memory. When drinking, he would sing and play with the kids. These were her only experiences with drunk people.

Mom was a tomboy growing up in the country but was the prettiest girl in high school, according to my father and a couple of uncles. They lived on a mountain named after a great, great grandfather in Walton. It was Droddy Mountain, their last name. I always pictured the television show "The Waltons" when she described it.

I never heard much about my parent's courtship and am unsure when my father's friendship with the woman he lived with ended. My mom told a story about my father coming to see her once, and they left with one of his friends, leaving my father's Model A Ford behind in my grandparent's yard. My uncle Dick gathered the local kids, mostly his siblings, and they would coast the Model A to the bottom of the mountain with Dick driving. Since they didn't have the key, they had to push it back up the hill, so Uncle Dick recruited them. They kept it up until they were too tired.

Mom told of another time when one of his friends was teasing her about being the best pitcher when the local kids played baseball. She threatened him with a rock. He stuck his head out from behind the tree where he hid, pointed to his nose, and said, "If you're so good, hit me here." She dropped him, giving him a bloody nose and two black eyes.

In July of 1940, my grandfather Droddy came home from work. On his way into the kitchen to say hello to my grandmother, he noticed my father and Mom sitting on the edge of a bed in the girl's bedroom. He instructed my grandmother to straighten their daughter out because he wouldn't tolerate that behavior. She informed him my parents had just returned from Madison, where they were married. My father's mom was their witness. My father was seventeen, my mom was sixteen, and neither had finished high school.

My parents didn't talk much about the time they were first married. My father said he drove a log truck for one dollar a day. I remember my mom talking about working in a department store, but I am unsure if that was during this time. I remember her discussing how much different my father was initially. She said he was kind, sweet, and attentive.

World War II was the thing that had a significant impact on my father and, as a result, the rest of us. Tensions had been building in the country when they married, but to them, the war in Europe was far away. That all changed in December of 1941 when the president declared war. The government had started the draft in September 1940 in a limited amount. Still, after Pearl Harbor, the numbers increased dramatically. In early 1942 my father was nineteen and though married, still had no kids. It isn't something my parents talked about directly. Still, I heard bits and pieces later of how my father was called a couple of times but tried to avoid it by getting what they called a deferment. He had always been smart, though his school record might not have shown it. And if the story of the broken egg on the bus and my mom's description of him at that time were correct, he must have been a sensitive kid. Having never seen that side of him, I can only imagine what it must have been like to be called up after the horror stories of WWI trench battles. He did get temporary deferments (at least one). My mom told stories of him doing nothing but crying in boot camp. Finally, he was taken and put on a ship to England.

As a terrified teenager, he managed to distinguish himself. By the time my sister was born in December of 1944, he was a sergeant leading a squad in the middle of the Battle of the Bulge. He was wounded and earned a Bronze Star when his squad was overrun. A kid of twenty years, he lay with shrapnel in his leg as the Germans approached, shooting and bayonetting anyone that moved. The only way he survived was to crawl beneath his dead friends and wait for the Germans to pass. Once it was clear, he picked up the mic of his nearby dead radioman. He called in his coordinates, notifying the Americans about the German location so they could bomb the enemy. Those minutes must have been terrifying. He woke up in a hospital in France from the friendly fire.

I learned all this when he was on another crying drunk because he usually never talked about the war and wouldn't even watch war movies on TV. He hated "that coward" John Wayne for staying home and making movies instead of volunteering while my father had to kick his own men's feet to make them mad so they would wake up and wouldn't freeze to death over there.

According to my mom, he returned a different man. The term PTSD didn't exist during the Second World War. The closest at the time was to say someone was "shell-shocked"; doctors usually reserved it for men who could not function. Since my father could carry on most days, they didn't consider him to have an impairment. The man who returned home was jumpy, moody, and had trouble sleeping because of nightmares. If my mom found him asleep, she would have to stand out of reach and call his name because touching him or standing too close would likely result in physical harm. During this period, he began to drink much more heavily and would stay out with a different crowd than he had before. They were men that liked to drink, fight and carouse, as my mom put it. He would come home drunk late at night and accuse my mom of cheating. When it got to where he began to hit her, my mom was not sure what to do. By this time, she was the mother of a young girl. Married at sixteen, she had not finished high school, so her job prospects were not good. This young girl, who had never heard her parents raise their voices, was unprepared for such anger and aggression.

Sometime during this period, she decided to end it all. She tells the story of how she mixed up some poison into two glasses of milk. She sat at the kitchen table with her young daughter, Rita my oldest sister, and instructed her to drink the milk. However, sitting there with her innocent child in her lap, she realized she could not do it, so she quickly packed up and left him. The separation lasted around three months. Struggling to pay bills and get an apartment, she was determined not to go back. He followed her and begged her to return, but she refused and threatened a restraining order. My mom's father told me a story several times about how they got back together. My father whined and pleaded not just with my mom but also with her parents. Grandpa Droddy said my father seemed so pitiful that he decided to discuss my father's case with my mom. When she asked him what she should do, he said that my father seemed genuinely sorry and that he deserved another chance. She reluctantly agreed to go back. My grandpa admitted he regretted having a hand in the whole thing. But then he smiled at me and tried to lighten the mood by saying that he wouldn't have had me around if he hadn't, and he was glad I was there.

My mother said my father was much better for a while and seemed almost to be his old loving, gentle self. My father, meanwhile, had learned to weld to support his growing family. Work was hard to find in West Virginia, and soon my parents were off to South Carolina, where my father found a job as a welder. My father also began to slip back into his previous behavior of drinking heavily, staying out, and being abusive to my mom. First verbally, then physically. My youngest sister, Annette, had been born by this time, and my mom was pregnant again. Now she felt utterly trapped in the marriage. She was a high school dropout, away from home with two children, and pregnant again. My brother, Ernest Jr, or Buddy, was born in South Carolina, and my mother felt that sealed her fate. They moved back to West Virginia, and I was born two years after my brother.

I often wondered about the gap between my sisters. My oldest sister was eight years older than my youngest sister, and only two years later, my brother arrived. Still, I never learned about any reason until much later in life, so I figured it was just how it was.

This was the world into which I was born.

Part Two

Childhood

Chapter 3

Gun!

I guess it is normal for some of your earliest memories to result from extreme emotions, either pleasant or unpleasant. My first memory was looking down the barrel of a real gun, a pistol my father held on my mother. That long moment is frozen in time forever for me. I was four or five years old, standing in the back bedroom of the trailer at the end of the hall that ran through the kids' bedroom and bathroom to my parent's room. I was on my mother's right side, with my left hand touching the back of her leg, just above the knee. My height made the pistol barrel fall precisely at eye level as my father held it, pointing at my mother's stomach. The gun was a .22 caliber revolver but looked like a cannon. It was less than two feet in front of me. I could have reached out and touched it! My brother was on my mother's other side, and my youngest sister was behind us. There is no memory of the fight that led up to the incident. It was a typical argument every weekend when my father came home drunk after going out for a pack of cigarettes.

There must have been some threat that alarmed us because all the children were around my mother. I recall my father's face the seconds before I realized there was a gun. He was leaning toward my mother, shouting. His face contorted in anger, hatred, and contempt for the woman before him. The veins and ligaments in his neck were visible to me below. I instinctively leaned away from the threat. I remember the feel of the bedspread on my right hand as I brushed against it.

My father accused my mother of cheating on him. My mother denied it and asked why he thought she would want anything to do with the person with whom he accused her of having an affair. Then the gun appeared! I was transfixed. I saw nothing but the pistol as I stood there waiting for it to go off. Sounds are the only memories recorded other than the gun barrel. I heard my father's drunken voice call my mother a whore. I never saw my mother look at another man and wondered how my father could get such an idea. I was sure he thought he should kill her based on the look of hatred on my father's face and the rage in his voice. I wanted to look for any softening in the glaring blue eyes of my father but could not take my eyes off the gun. I remember my sister screaming, "No, daddy, please don't!" as she began to cry.

Suddenly my mother stiffened. I could tell because I had moved to cling to her leg when I saw the gun. "Go ahead and shoot me then, you son-of-a-bitch! I'm not gonna lie and confess to something I didn't do."

I couldn't believe it! What was she saying? What was she doing? I was sure that this would put my father over the edge. I wanted to scream, tell her to shut up and ask her if she was crazy. I wanted to run, so I didn't see what I was sure would happen. But no shout would come. I couldn't run. All I could do was witness my mother's imminent death. I felt so powerless, so helpless, so frightened, and so angry.

My mother continued. "Go ahead! I'd be better off." A pause either for effect or because she saw him softening. "I'd be better off dead than to live the way I do." Another pause. "So go ahead and shoot. You'd be doing me a favor."

I do not remember how the situation de-escalated. There is a version of my father saying she wasn't worth going to prison, but I do not remember if someone told me that later. I don't recall because a greater, more devastating one replaced the fear of the gun. My mother would rather be dead than live her life the way it was. I thought of all the times my mother sat at home, watching supper growing colder and getting more upset by the minute. Did she mean that?

Does she want to die and leave me and my brother and sisters? Could I possibly be part of the reason? I had heard her tell people that she would leave if it weren't for the kids. Was it my fault that she was stuck with my father? After all, I was the youngest, so I would keep her there the longest. If it weren't for me, she might be happy somewhere else.

Chapter 4

I Saw Santa!

The trailer park where we lived was called Fair Winds Trailer Park. They frequently seemed to have exotic names. We had a significant snowstorm one Christmas Eve. I can remember because of two things. That afternoon, all the kids, with my mother, built a snowman that must have been six or seven feet tall. As a small child, I remember standing there looking up at it, and it seemed as tall as our trailer to me. We found stones to make the buttons, eyes, and mouth; my mom even donated a carrot for the nose. It stood like a sentinel at the front of our trailer, beside the sidewalk to the front door. I was amazed, and even when we had to go inside, I kept staring at it through the window. When it came time for dinner, they dragged me to the table, and I quickly ate because I could not see him from my chair, though not for lack of trying. I began to worry a little, and I think my mother could tell because she asked me what was wrong.

"Do you think that the snowman will scare Santa's reindeer?" I asked.

"No. Of course not. Even reindeer like snowmen," my mom assured me.

By the time dinner was finished, it was dark out, and it was hard to see the snowman even with the Christmas lights on the outside of the trailer, so I eventually became distracted. Then the big news hit! We were watching the local news on TV when they announced that someone had spotted Santa's sleigh over the state of Delaware! They showed a live picture of it from a shopping center we knew was close, so we all ran outside.

It was a cold clear night with few clouds in the sky, and we all scanned to find Santa. I have to admit that I was somewhat distracted by the snowman. He was an imposing figure to me in the dark and, frankly, just a bit scary. I pretended I was looking for the sleigh but kept the snowman in my peripheral vision.

Suddenly I heard my oldest sister, Ritzie ,exclaim, "There he Is! There's Santa!" As she pointed in the opposite direction from the snowman. Screams of delight from my younger sister, Annette, and brother, Buddy, as they honed in on him. I was still having trouble locating him because I couldn't see over my siblings, so Ritzie, who would have been in her mid-teens at the time, picked me up. I could just make out some red lights first, then what looked like a sleigh with a tiny man in a red suit. "Is that him?" I asked, pointing at the small object in the sky.

"Yes, Mike. That's Santa!" my mom answered as I joined in the screaming. He was far away, and I only managed a glimpse before he disappeared, but it sure looked like it could be Santa to me.

Not missing a beat, my mom insisted that we hurry up and get ready for bed if he was so close. She had no trouble herding us in the trailer to get our baths and get to bed that Christmas Eve, though I remember trying to stay awake to listen for the reindeer on the roof. I was sure I would hear them since our bunkbed was close to the ceiling. I knew Santa was real because I saw him. And it may have caused me to keep believing even after some other kids my age began doubting. I mean, you have to believe your own eyes.

Chapter 5

Holidays

Holidays, in general, were dreaded because my father would always get drunk, and then my parents would fight. I remember many Christmas mornings when I would wake up excited to see what Santa had brought me. I would lie awake, waiting to hear anyone else stirring in the house, sure that I would get in trouble if I climbed out of bed too early. When the others finally got up, usually my older sister or mom, I would fly into the living room where the tree stood in the corner. I would stand nearby and look at all the presents under the tree. The larger ones would always catch my eye first, and I would strain to see if I could read the tags, hoping they were for me. You must keep a respectable distance; otherwise, you risk the wrath of my parents. I could always spot the bags of candy, nuts, and oranges my mom used to make the tree look more bountiful, and I quickly discounted them. The fake volume wasn't fooling me.

Our practice was always to wait until everyone was up, which was torture. Then we took turns from year to year handing out all the presents. We would then take turns opening one at a time. I knew this was contrived to make children suffer as long as possible.

When we distributed everything, and you saw how few you received, it quickly lost a bit of its thrill. It was also easy to determine, once again, the Sting Ray bicycle had not made the cut this year from the shape of the presents in my pile. I later learned from my mother what a battle it was every year to get almost any money from my father to buy gifts. She religiously saved all the S&H Green Stamps to augment our presents as much as possible. I rarely remember getting very many things on my list and was often reminded by both parents and siblings to be grateful for what I did receive. Lots of poor kids in the world got nothing. Any article of clothing was viewed as a rip-off as they were necessities and certainly not toys. Every year things like underwear, socks, and mittens managed to dilute my Christmas haul even further.

My mom made us endure breakfast first before going outside to play with new toys or, even better, to find out what our friends received. Once nourished, we would usually bolt out the door for three reasons. The first was to play with the new stuff. The second was to head to my friend's house immediately, and the third was to get out of sight and range before my father got drunk. We would stay out as long as possible, only returning when we knew it was dinner time, as attendance at Christmas dinner was required. We cautiously approached the place to see if my father was even home. If not, it was both good and bad news. It was good because we could talk our mom into letting us eat anyway and enjoy a peaceful meal without him. It was also bad since we knew it likely meant a worse fight later because he had missed the Christmas meal.

If his car was there, meant he was home, so we would approach slowly to see if we could hear any arguing. If so, we might dally outside, just out of sight, until my mom came out and called for us to come and eat.

Meals, when my father was drunk, were filled with tension. The outcome was always unpredictable. The kids waited until he served himself to ensure we didn't take a piece of something he had wanted or too much. He would often want to be waited on, so he would ask one of us to make him a plate. He might ask any of us some inane question that may or may not make sense or intentionally try to embarrass one of us for his entertainment. He may try to continue some argument with my mom by commenting on the meal or making one of us the target of his anger to annoy our mother. This tactic would usually prompt her to swoop in to protect us and confront him. Her confrontation would result in anything from him laughing it off to throwing a plate of food at her or the wall. The living room's front wall had a slice in the blonde wood paneling from where a dinner plate had impaled it years ago. Holidays usually concluded in one of three ways. He would get mad and leave again, driving off and not returning until the wee hours. He would retreat to the bathroom where he kept his Kentucky Gentleman bourbon to brace and recharge himself so the battle could continue, or he would, hopefully, lie down and sleep it off for the rest of the night if he were drunk enough. We hoped for the last one, but it could also quickly escalate to violence when he was so intoxicated.

If he did storm out, the rest of the evening was tense, listening for his car to return, knowing that if he returned while we were up, anyone of us could be a target for verbal or physical abuse, though usually it was directed at my mother. If he came in later, we all pretended to be asleep, which sometimes spared us but not always since he had to go through our bedroom to reach theirs. He might stop and rant in the middle of our room or, heaven forbid, sit down on the edge of the bed to try to awaken us. Ignoring a raging drunk less than three feet away from you while pretending to be asleep is very stressful. Even after he went to bed, I would strain to listen and ensure they weren't fighting in their room because it usually erupted into a full-blown battle.

It didn't matter the holiday, the agenda, other than opening presents, was always the same. Most weekends from the time I was about ten were similar. My brother and I would try to get up and get out of the house before he had time to take his first drink. I learned to appreciate pop-tarts because they could be warmed in a toaster and eaten on the run. Dressed, breakfast made, and out the door within ten minutes. We would cruise by at a safe distance around lunchtime, and if clear, meaning his car was gone, we would run in for a quick sandwich. We would blast back out and not return until supper.

Chapter 6

If I Don't Die, My Parents Will Surely Kill Me

The street in our trailer park was a big circle that led back to the entrance. When you first came into the complex, if you turned right, you would go down a hill that dropped somewhat sharply, at least in my memory. All the kids in the neighborhood loved this hill, and we would gather there to ride our bicycles, tricycles, wagons, and scooters down the incline so that we could go really fast. Our mom hammered into us to be careful and respectful of cars, so we didn't cause trouble, get hurt, or get killed.

One particular Saturday, we were all there as usual. The year was around 1960, and I was only four years old, so I rode a tricycle. I had just reached the top of the hill, which took some effort on a tricycle. I was looking forward to the ride down to feel the wind on my face. It was a brisk fall day, and I was wearing a sweater and one of those caps with ear flaps to keep my ears warm. The flaps were up on the climb up the hill, and I was hot from the exertion. I was lining up to take off when I heard one of the kids yell, "Car coming!" We all scrambled to the side of the street for safety.

A man and woman were in the car, and they stopped, asking if we knew where some person lived. It must have been an adult because all of us kids just shook our heads no. The man thanked us, and they proceeded slowly down the hill. I remember watching the big chrome bumper of the 1950's era sedan lumber down the incline because the top was right at my eye level. I was impatient since I was hot and anxious to get moving, but we all dutifully waited until the car reached the bottom of the hill. As soon as it did, we were off. I remember looking up at the kid on a bicycle beside me as we took off. Leaning into the handlebars, I was determined to pick up as much speed as possible, even though I knew the kid on the bike would be much faster than me. I figured that if he turned around and I was right behind him, he would still be impressed that a tricycle had stayed that close to him.

As I glanced over to see where he was relative to me, I noticed that he was scrambling to get his feet back on his bike pedals. He must have been worried that I was still beside him. We were halfway down the hill by this time, and I was going full tilt. Then, I heard the squeal of his back tire, and I looked over to see him slamming on his brakes by moving the pedal backward to activate the coaster brakes. What was he doing? At the same time, I heard him scream, "Car!" He steered his bike sideways as the back tires smoked slightly from the braking.

Looking forward again, I saw why he panicked. At the bottom of the hill, that nice man had stopped to ask an adult on the sidewalk something, probably about the person he was trying to find. I was going full speed on a tricycle and closing fast on the back bumper of a late '50s Buick. All I could see was a horizon of chrome. It was like a wall coming at me. I tried frantically to get my feet on the pedals to slow myself. It was no luck, as they were a blur of motion. If I wanted to turn, getting my feet on them would be even harder because it would make the outside one farther away, and the inside foot could go into the spokes.

It was one of those occasions where time seemed to slow down. The bumper was so shiny that I could see myself flying toward this mass of chrome, sure that I would die. I mean, I figured I must have been going at least one hundred, right? I thought about how painful it would be to be smashed like a bug on the back of a Buick. How sad my parents would be when I was dead. Well, at least my mom.

Then a worse thought crept in. What if I live? I would be in BIG trouble for running into the back of someone's car. I pictured the whole rear end of the big car crumpled from the impact. The guy getting out and coming after me for the damage I had done. Would he beat up some poor, bloodied kid, picking me up off the road to slap me around? Oh man, how would I ever pay for it? I heard Buicks were expensive cars.

I tried again, the pedals slapping at the bottom of my shoes. No way could I get my feet synched in time. I didn't think my legs could pedal that fast. I could see myself clearly in the bumper now, see my eyes wide with fear. Hopefully, I would die. First, the driver would slap me around for crashing his car. Then my parents would kill me for being so stupid if I lived—especially my dad. I was sure that he hated me, anyway. It would be just one more reason for him to justify killing me. I glanced up at the taillights and prayed that the man would let off the brake and take off down the street. Aren't Buicks powerful and fast? Maybe I would miss him.

No, I was going so fast now that there was no way that he could get out of the way. I was flying. It could be a new land speed record for a tricycle. What a brave kid I would be to die while setting a new record in the process. I hoped that's how they would remember me. Maybe there would be parades, and my mom wouldn't be so sad knowing her son was now a hero. Ticker tape flashed before me, with a long line of cars, the crowd cheering from the sidewalks, and my mom, so proud, holding up a big picture of me for everyone to see.

Flooded with fear, the wind in my face, I reached up with one hand and flipped down my ear flaps, hoping the faux-leather outside would protect my head and ears. I pictured a fighter pilot zipping through the sky during the old biplane era. I must be going at least that fast. The deadly impact was eminent now, my vision filled with chrome and the slight hint of exhaust in my nose. I braced for impact by leaning back to protect my head and locking my elbows; sure this was the end.

Bong!

My handlebars hit the bumper on the driver's side. I rose off the seat, but my sneakers caught the back platform of the tricycle, my nose inches from the trunk lid. The bill of my cap covered my eyes. There was collective breath-holding from the crowd of kids as the driver's door opened. I sat there stunned. Would he grab me and march me down the street, demanding to speak to the parents of this little juvenile delinquent?

"Are you okay, Sport?" was all he said.

I was afraid to say anything. I just sat there, still holding on to the handlebars for dear life. I saw him glance at the bumper. I finally managed to perceive the bumper instead of a wall of chrome. Not a scratch. You couldn't tell I had touched it.

He touched my shoulder. "Hey..."

"Please don't tell," I pleaded.

"Don't worry. Look, you didn't even scratch it." He pointed at the mass of Detroit steel in front of us. "I'm just glad you're okay."

"Thanks, mister." I could feel my eyes welling with tears, so I looked away. I'm unsure if it was from fear, relief, or the intensity of what I had just experienced.

"I remember what it was like to be a kid. You just be more careful from now on, okay?" He smiled and helped me move over to the sidewalk with the trike.

I watched him get back in his car and drive away, waving. I felt a little better when he passed our trailer, but I couldn't help the tears streaming down my face. My brother and youngest sister caught up to me about that time. I was sure that one of them would tell, or maybe the adult who had given the man directions. I lived on pins and needles for a few days, but the shoe never dropped. Everyone kept my secret.

Chapter 7

There are Mean People in the World

I am unsure where they came from, but my brother and I acquired two dogs. I think they came from a local flea market called the Farmer's Market, but I can't imagine my father paying money for a dog. In any case, in a rare moment of humanity, or perhaps of drunken sentimentalism, my father allowed Buddy and I to each get a dog. They were both short-haired terrier/hound mixes and both female. My brother named his Ginger, and my dog was Cha-cha. I am not sure where that name came from, but given my age, at the time, I assume that I had only recently heard the word and thought it sounded cool, so that's what I called her.

They were relatively unremarkable dogs in that I don't remember much about them other than they were ours and a healthy competition between my brother and me trying to teach them tricks. Given the age difference, my brother probably was the better trainer or at least convinced me of it. I am unsure of the circumstances that led up to the events, but at some point, at least one of the dogs became pregnant. I remember being disappointed that we could not keep all the puppies. My brother and I would occasionally get lax about walking the dogs, turning them loose to wander a bit.

The pregnancy fascinated me, and I remember trying to be gentle with the mothers. To my surprise, one morning, I awoke to find they had delivered four puppies, and as I watched them rooting about, barely able to crawl with their eyes not yet open, I heard my mom say, look, there's another one coming. With both horror and fascination, I witnessed the mother squeezing out the fifth puppy and then licking it to clean it. My brother and I helped take care of the puppies until they were of age, occasionally getting scolded for handling them too much. When they were six weeks, they were put in a box and taken to be given away. I was sad to see them go, but everyone assured me they would be too much for us to manage. At least, that was what our parents told us.

Not long after this, my brother tried to feed our dogs, and neither seemed interested in eating. They had been acting unusual all afternoon and remained in bed when he called them. Usually, they stumbled all over each other to see who could get to the food first. My brother took a bit of food over to his dog Ginger, trying to tempt her to get up and eat. She showed very little interest in the food. Cha-cha raised her head but then whined and laid back down.

Worried she could grow weak from not eating, he put his hands under her body and tried to help her up to her feet. Ginger let out a sharp yelp, then a whimper, and I heard my brother gasp.

"Mom," my brother said, half question and half pleading. Blood ran out of her mouth and anus when he lifted the dog. My brother was scared that he had done something wrong. My mother got my father's attention, then took the dog from my brother and wrapped her in a towel. She also checked on Cha-cha. My father came over and took a look at the dogs. I could tell by his expression that it was not good. They had a brief discussion, with my mother insisting my father take them to the vet. My father reluctantly agreed. He was not the type of person to spend money on a vet when you could find a stray dog anywhere, but because it was a weeknight and he wasn't drinking, my mother managed to prevail. They placed both dogs in the car and told my brother and me to stay home. There was a tearful departure as we tried to follow them out to the car, my mother sitting in the back with both dogs.

We waited not so patiently for any word or for our parents to reappear with our pets. Our older sisters tried to distract us with little effect until, finally, our parents returned. We watched them walk in from the car with neither dog in tow.

"Maybe they had to stay at the vet overnight," Buddy suggested. I was terrified but tried to convince myself he was right. I wondered what could happen that would make them both sick simultaneously.

My parents came in, and my mom sat us on the couch and told us our dogs were gone. They did not make it.

Between sobs, we both asked the same thing, "Why?"

Not being the most patient parent in the world, my father blurted out simply, "Because that son-of-a-bitch down at the end fed them glass in hamburger, that's why. That bastard, I'm gonna." Another sharp look from my mom. "It tore their whole insides up."

My brother and I were speechless, and I heard my sister behind us gasp. Mom shot my father a dirty look. He just threw up his hands and walked back into the bathroom. We could hear him enter the closet, where he kept his whiskey. He was pouring himself a drink. Great.

"Why would someone do that?" I asked.

"Well, honey, I guess some people don't like dogs. And when the dogs run loose, they do things to hurt them. There are some mean people in the world."

I cried myself to sleep that night, thinking about how much it must have hurt our poor dogs to have died that way. I was also frightened that people would put ground glass in a hamburger and feed it to an unsuspecting animal. What would they do to a kid? How could someone be that cruel? I wanted to do something to hurt that person to make them pay for it. I wondered if we could call the cops and have them arrested. Mostly I missed our sweet dogs and grieved their horrible deaths. I have no idea if my father exacted any kind of revenge, but I know I stayed away from the yard of the man my father accused. It was a hard lesson for two young boys to learn, and I always felt guilty for letting our dogs run loose.

Chapter 8

First Lesson in Economics

As I described earlier, the trailer park was a circle, and when you entered the park, we were on the row that would be to the right, on the inside of the ring. There were trailers on the outside of that row, also. On the other side of the circle, behind us, there were only trailers on the inside. Midway on the outside of the ring on that side was a cinderblock building. One part of the building held some machinery I don't remember, perhaps a well. The other half of the building contained a laundry mat the residents could use. I would go with my mom occasionally when she put laundry in or go to take it out. It was close to the back of our trailer, so she would start loads and then go back home to do things.

On the outside of the building was a Pepsi vending machine. It was one of the first vending machines I ever saw that held cans because most them held bottles. They would have a door on the left that you could open, and a column of bottles was locked in place. Once you put in your coin, it would unlock the mechanism, allowing only one to dispense. They designed it so you couldn't pull more than one at a time. However, this machine had buttons that displayed the types of soda, and when you put in your coin(s) and made your selection, you would hear a clunk, and your drink would drop into a tray at the bottom of the machine.

At the time, the drinks were only a dime for a twelve-ounce can of Pepsi, and whenever I got my hands on a dime, I was a frequent customer. I learned from my brother to go into the laundry, check around the machines for any dropped coins, and check the pay phone outside the building for unclaimed coins. We would be proud of our diligence when we stumbled on any money left behind.

I remember being alone once, which was unusual and probably resulted from my brother not wanting me to follow him around. Out of complete boredom, I checked the payphone for any loot. It was rare that I found anything, mainly because my brother, who was two years older, would always beat me to the phone. This time though, I hit pay dirt. A whole quarter! I remember holding it in my hand and wishing I had someone to witness this great victory. I knew my brother wouldn't believe me. I looked around to see if anyone saw me. No other kids were out for me to call over with whom to celebrate. Oh well, I would enjoy it all by myself. I walked to the Pepsi machine and tried to insert my prize.

It didn't fit. I looked at the quarter and the slot. It was only big enough for a dime. Crap! I couldn't go home and ask my mom because she probably wouldn't want me spending my money on a soda. Maybe I could ask some other adult, but who? I looked across the street. A few trailers to my left was a nice lady I had met. She and my mom were friends, and her name was Mrs. Bryant. I think she was also from the south, Virginia, so she and my mom bonded. I had sat at her kitchen table while she and my mom drank coffee and visited, and she had commented on what a good boy I was.

I took off at a run, around the corner of her trailer and up the steps. The open front door was a sign that she was home, and I lightly rapped on the screen door.

"Well, hello, Mike. What a nice surprise. Is your mom coming?" she said as she opened the screen. She was older than my mom and still had the drawl that revealed her region of origin.

"No, ma'am. She's at home."

"Well, what can I do for you? Would you like a drink of water or something?"

"I was wondering if you could help me."

"I will if I can. What do you need, Darling?"

I held up the quarter so she could see it. "I have this quarter, and I was gonna get a Pepsi, but it won't fit in the machine. Would you trade me a dime for it?"

She chuckled and said, "No, but I'll give you two dimes and a nickel for it."

"Really?!" I had no idea about the relative value of money and wondered if I was taking advantage of the nice lady.

"Yes," she let me in, and we entered her kitchen, where she had her purse on the table. Opening her change purse, she counted out the coins, and we made the exchange. "Now, a dime is worth ten pennies, and a nickel is worth five. So how much does that make a quarter worth?"

"Two dimes and a nickel?" I answered based on what she had previously said.

"Yes. But how many pennies is that?"

"Uh." Is this a trick question, I wondered.

"How far can you count?"

"My sister taught me to count to a hundred." I was sure that would impress her.

"How old are you now?" she asked.

I had two dimes and a nickel burning a hole in my pocket and was not sure what this had to do with anything. "I'm four," I said, holding up my fingers to show her.

"Well, maybe arithmetic is a little advanced for you, then. Okay?"

"Okay." I sensed that the transaction might be drawing to a close. "Thank you for helping me," I said as I approached the door.

"Don't spend it all on Pepsi's."

"I won't." I walked to the front of her trailer, then sprinted back to the Pepsi machine, hoping she wouldn't call my mom.

Chapter 9

Studying for the Interview

My father quit high school after the tenth grade, but he was by no means stupid. He worked most of his life as a welder in the shipyards during World War II, continuing to do so both before and after his service. They had moved to work at the Newport News Shipyards in Virginia during the war and briefly in Wilmington, Delaware. After the war, he found a job in South Carolina, where my brother was born in 1954. But by 1956, when I was born, they were back in West Virginia. They had moved to Delaware in 1960, so my father could find work, but he decided he would have more options if he branched out. He had heard that DuPont was hiring but did not need welders. They were looking for pipe fitters to help with their chemical manufacturing plant in Deepwater, New Jersey.

Wanting to find more stable work, my father decided to apply as a pipe fitter. He found a book on pipe fitting and locked himself in my parent's bedroom for several days, having lined up an interview the following Monday morning. I remember bits and pieces about it because it was such unusual behavior, and I remember Mom telling us to go out and play and to be quiet because my father was studying.

I wondered why an adult would need to learn, but I did as instructed. We only saw him at supper that weekend. He even took his lunch in the back bedroom studying. After his weekend of intense cramming, my father went to the interview and aced it. He got a job that would pay more and also have benefits. It would be steady work allowing us to remain in one place longer. I just knew that my parents were greatly relieved and excited. He did well at DuPont until he took a medical retirement in the mid-1970s.

Chapter 10

The Soup Can Story

Families often have stories passed down from sibling to sibling to educate or indoctrinate the younger. These are often stories of daring-do by those who have preceded them. Other times they are stories of caution or hard lessons learned and passed down to prevent the younger children from making the same possibly life-threatening mistakes. The following story was both legend and a tale of caution for the young siblings in our family.

During this period, my oldest sister, Ritzie, who was twelve years older, hit her sixteenth birthday and had grown to about five feet, four inches tall. My mother was only five foot two. One day my mother was standing at the stove, getting ready to make a can of soup for lunch, when my sister came walking past her, heading out the front door, noting to herself proudly that her eye level now came to the top of my mom's head. As you came in, the trailer entrance was between the living room in the front and the kitchen/dining room just to the left. My mother told my sister that she needed to take out the trash.

It has been lost to history whether my sister was kidding with my mother, but since she was on her way to some destination, my sister remarked, "I don't have to, 'cause I'm bigger than you now."

The next thing my sister knew, she picked herself up off the floor with a splitting headache. Mom, who was about to open the can of Campbell's soup, grabbed it and hit my sister in the head with the side of the can, knocking her to the floor.

My mom stood over her, saying, "When I tell you to do something, you don't backtalk me, girl."

"Yes, ma'am," my sister managed to answer, holding her head and trying to steady herself. She felt for blood, sure that her skull was fractured. Since my mom had hit her with the side of the can, it didn't break the skin. It did produce a pronounced knot. Once she felt good enough to move again, she went straight to the trash can and emptied it.

I do not claim this story is absolutely true, but it was passed down to me by my older sisters with solemn reassurances and hearts crossed that it was a fact. It was a compelling story that taught a valuable lesson. Do NOT backtalk your mother, and always do what she tells you. My mother rarely ever had to give threats or tell us twice to do something. We might joke with her about doing it later, from a distance. Still, one flash of my mother's eyes and the setting of her jaw would produce rapid assurances that the offending party was just kidding, along with immediate action. This was true until we each moved out and even continued into adulthood.

Chapter 11

Is That My Dad?

The last episode I remember when we lived in Delaware was my father's fistfight with one of his cousins. I remember this cousin's name was David, and he was from "back home" in West Virginia. I was not in school yet, so that I would have been four or five years old. Mom told me later that the fight started over my oldest sister. She wanted to go to a dance at the high school, and my father had denied her permission to go. My father was sure her goal was to have sex with some boy, and he was having none of it. She may have told the cousin she had nothing to wear anyway, so it didn't matter.

He was staying with us for a visit and possibly looking for work. It had been a pleasant day, and we younger children, including Annette, Buddy, and I, had already taken our bath and were in bed. David must have appealed to my father to let my sister go to the dance. My father told him to mind his own business. David even suggested that he would pay for a dress for my sister. My father then accused him of having unclean thoughts about my sister, and the words escalated. It wasn't long before it became physical.

They had been sitting at the kitchen table when it started, which was just on the other side of the thin veneer wall of our bedroom. I was so young that I only remember flashes of a few things, but I remember my mom and sister screaming at them to break it up and David yelling that he would give my father what he deserved. My brother and I huddled in the bunk bed in the kids' bedroom. We were about five feet off the floor and behind a wooden railing that protected us from rolling out of the top bed, peeking out beneath the railing, trying to see what was happening.

We heard the struggle in the other room and were frightened it would come into the bedroom. At one point, we saw my father dash to the back bedroom where my parent's slept. The hallway ran right through the middle of the bedroom, with a closet and built-in drawers on one side and the beds on the other, so they passed within two feet of the beds. Knowing my father, I can only assume that he was trying to gain access to the pistol he kept back there. He was followed closely by his cousin in hot pursuit.

I could hear Annette whimpering in the bed below us, and she screamed, "Daddy!" as he ran past. We could then hear the struggle continue in my parent's bedroom, which was just on the other side of the tiny bathroom that was the width of a bathtub. So, there were only about eight feet and two thin walls between us and the fight.

Within a few minutes, we were surprised to see my father run into our room and slam the pocket door closed behind him. I don't think my father had time to get his pistol because he kept it locked in a small drop-leaf desk in their bedroom. He wouldn't have had time to locate the key and open the lock before David followed him.,

My youngest sister had a small, blue child's rocking chair that sat in the tiny space on the floor between the bottom bed and the hallway. My father quickly grabbed the rocking chair, jumped on the foot of the bottom bed, and held the chair above his head by the two spindles of the back. The chair was right at our level as we cringed in the bunk. It was only about eighteen inches wide. One of the flashes, I remember the back of my father's head as he slightly stooped to make room for the chair over his head. I could see the curve of the runners and how blue paint had chipped off them from rubbing on the floor.

We heard David come running down the hallway and fumble with the door slamming it open. He then started to sprint through the bedroom, chasing my father. As David went through the door, my father brought the chair down, splintering it on his head. I watched it as the slats burst and twisted with finishing nails sticking out, and David stumbled, then collapsed in the doorway between the kitchen sink and the bedroom. My father shot past him into the kitchen and turned to face him.

As David struggled to recover, his hands found the kitchen countertop and a beer bottle someone had set near the sink. He grabbed it by the neck and smashed it against the counter, holding the jagged top like a knife. Then he lunged out of sight, taking a swing at my father with the improvised weapon. David was screaming incomprehensibly as the two men struggled on the kitchen floor.

I was sure my father would be cut to pieces, and my mother and Ritzie were screaming again. I have no idea how long the struggle lasted, but I heard the front door slam open at some point and could hear a siren as it approached. It grew quiet in the house. Buddy and I climbed down from the bunk and peeked around the doorway with Annette. Ritzie was near the front door and waved to us, indicating it was okay. I could hear a commotion outside as the police tried to subdue David.

They found him between our trailer and the neighbors behind us. He had gone crazy from the blow to the head and was taking out his anger by putting his fist through the bottom of a flat-bottomed rowboat our neighbor's owned. They eventually had to tranquilize him and remove him in a straight-jacket.

The three of us moved tentatively into the living room, where my mother was attending to someone in the lounge chair. The other image burned into my memory is the person with a blood-covered face cut so bad that their eyes were swollen almost shut. I heard my sister ask, "Daddy?" When I looked back again, I couldn't recognize him, but I saw the skin lying open and my mother trying to staunch the bleeding with a wet washcloth. I could only identify him by his auburn hair and the clothing I knew he had been wearing, though his shirt was ripped open and his t-shirt soaked in blood. He sat there trying to catch his breath and letting my mom attend to his wounds until an EMT arrived and took over.

I remember the mix of emotions that ran through me then. I remember worrying that my father would die, and I wondered what would happen to us. I wondered if my mom and we kids would be able to make it, and I thought it might be a chance to get rid of him, but I remembered my mom talking about how she never finished high school and had no job skills. I wanted both the ambulance guys to fix him and the police to take him away.

We had a new drama to worry about within a few days because we received notice that we had to move out of that trailer park. They would not tolerate fighting and having the police frequently show up. I wondered where we would go. What about all my friends? Couldn't they just make my dad move out? He was the troublemaker.

Chapter 12

Learning to Ride a Bicycle

Around this time, my father had traded his old panel truck that he used for a 1954 Chevy 3100 flatbed dually. It was dark green with a white grill. Designed for hauling and towing, it had a very low first gear my father called the mule gear. He fabricated a new flatbed out of some three-inch pipe for the frame and sheet metal, then fashioned wooden saddle bags to carry his tools. The welder and his acetylene tanks were in the middle. With this truck, he could move our mobile home himself. He occasionally took side jobs moving other mobile homes with my Uncle Dick. He also took on welding jobs on the weekends. Before I knew it, we had moved to the state of New Jersey across the Delaware River so my dad could be closer to his work. The new trailer park was only about a quarter mile from the front gate of the DuPont factory where he worked. It was a small trailer park, and we only lived there for about two years, so I don't remember much about it except learning to ride a bike.

This trailer park was in a horseshoe shape but with one small lane that intersected the two sides of the horseshoe. Our trailer was straight back, at the end of the right side as you entered, the second trailer in from the side. My oldest sister had her license, so my uncle helped her buy a car. It was a two-toned green Dodge Coronet. As I said earlier, she was twelve years older than me, so I would have been almost six. My youngest sister had a big 26-inch clunky girl's bicycle. It was blue, and I remember it had a big chrome spring right in front of the handlebars that provided some suspension for the bike. It also made the bike pretty heavy. Since it didn't have a crossbar like a boy's bike, I could climb up and sit on the seat. I remember my sister holding me up by the back of the seat and the handlebar and running beside me to get me started. Since the park had paved lanes, she let me go, and I was alone.

Suddenly, I was flying three feet off the ground, almost my entire height. I remember the sense of freedom, the breeze on my face, and the pavement sliding past as I steered the clunky blue bike to keep it away from the cars parked along the lane. Immediately, I was hooked on the sensation of movement. I looked down as I went over a bump, watching the action of the spring contract then expand. I could see the tread of the big fat tire spinning and then disappearing behind the front fender, the blur of the spokes. Steering and balance came naturally to me. I had no trouble avoiding obstacles and wanted to do this forever. What a joy to feel this free and enjoy the breeze and the warm sun on my face.

In the background, my sister's voice came through my reverie. I heard my name and then an excited exclamation. She was as excited as I was to witness this miracle of motion, like the first flight of a baby bird, the birth of my freedom. My brain didn't quite register the words other than my name. In my head, I translated it to "Fly, Mike, fly!" A smile spread across my face at my sister's pride in me.

Soon the front of the bike became sluggish and heavy. Its motion became labored and unsteady. An uncontrollable weave developed as my weight shifted to look behind me. I fought with the handlebars to keep them going in the intended direction, but the heavy monster seemed to have a mind of its own. Unsure what was wrong, I quickly glanced back at my sister for any hint of the problem's nature and how to correct it. Suddenly, my sister's words became clear, "Pedal, Mike, pedal!" I glanced over at my brother sitting on his bike, also yelling as I realized my mistake.

I fought to get my feet situated and moving in the right direction. I sensed I was fighting against the bike, as the front wheel was now almost perpendicular to my body. I sat momentarily suspended and saw the look of absolute disapproval and embarrassment on my brother's face. How could I have forgotten to pedal? What a dope he must think I am. I wonder how many people are watching my utter humiliation as I failed to master the basics of bicycle riding. I'll probably damage my sister's bike, so she'll never let me try again, reminding me of this disaster.

Now they were yelling something else. "Put your feet down!" My feet were diligently straining at the pedals, trying to recover as if glued to them. As I wobbled back and forth, I considered jumping off the seat, straddling the thing, and stopping it. Still, given my height relative to the seat and the monster's weight, it would probably just run over me. I had to ride it out.

Within seconds, all forward momentum was lost. The unstable beast fell on its side, the centrifugal force increasing as my head accelerated toward the ground. This was 1961, and there were no bicycle helmets, so my forehead bounced off the blacktop, and my knees ground into the rough surface under the bike's weight.

I looked up to see my sister running toward me with a look of horror on her face. I was sure she was going to hit me for crashing her bike. I heard my brother over my shoulder saying, "Why didn't you pedal, stupid?" I would get no sympathy from him or protection from my sister. I did what any five-and-a-half-year-old would do and began crying as if my life depended on it. My knee and head hurt, and I was sure I would die at her hand because my leg was still trapped beneath the behemoth.

"Are you okay, Mike? Are you okay," my sister said as she came running up. She lifted the bike off me and tossed it down on its other side, assessing my wounds. I looked at the big blue bike. Not a scratch on it. She was worried about getting in trouble with mom. I tried to be brave and reassure her I was okay between gulps of air. She walked me home and returned for the bike, telling me, "You did good balancing, but you've got to pedal to keep it going. You were steering and everything."

A few days later, after being patched up and slathered in that potion from the devil himself, mercurochrome, by my mom, I tried again on my brother's twenty-inch bike. With both him in my ear as he ran along and the voice in my head reminding me, I pedaled my little heart out and lapped the park three times before I returned the bike. This began my lifelong love of things two-wheeled and a decade-long battle between my brother and me to ensure equal time on shared two-wheelers.

Chapter 13

Starting School

I remember sitting on the trailer's front steps with my older sister. To be honest, I am not sure which one because they both used to teach me how to count and my ABCs. It must have been during the summer before my first year of school because I counted to one hundred, and my sister pronounced me ready. We were facing the trailer's front, which pointed west. Just as she said that I looked down at my arm. The sun peeked under the awning on the front of the trailer, warming my skin. It was like I was given a sign of a warm future with education.

It was the first time I was proud of myself for something, thanks to the praises of my sister. I had been engrained to know all my letters and how to count to one hundred before I started school so that the teachers wouldn't think I was some dummy. This must have come from my sister because I have no memory of my parents saying anything about scholastic achievements in a good or bad way.

I was terrified of leaving my mom behind as the bus pulled away, and my sister comforted me. Thanks to my sisters' encouragement, I was also confident in my abilities. We were bused to schools about five miles away, even though an elementary school was not a mile from our trailer park. It resulted from arbitrary school district boundaries that ended one street from our home. I thought it was dumb because I would have been able to run home from the other one if I got frightened. I was not afraid for myself but worried that something would happen to my mother. Perhaps my father would sneak out of work and kill her. I was sure he was capable ever since the incident with the gun. This fear would grow and worsen over the years of my elementary school days.

Two schools sat side by side where we first attended, splitting the elementary grades. I attended Pershing school, named for a general in World War I. The other was Lafayette, a general in the revolutionary war. Since my brother was two years older, he went to Lafayette, and I went to Pershing. I had hoped we would be in the same school, but knowing he was right next door was somewhat comforting. Since my younger sister was two years older than him, she was there too for fifth grade. We went there such a short time that not much else has stayed with me about the school.

Chapter 14

Another Move

It was another weekend, only a month after school started, and my father was drinking as always. I was likely playing out in the yard or doing some kid thing because I have no idea how it started. Still, suddenly Ritzie burst out the trailer's front door, yelling at the top of her voice. She was standing on the walkway in our yard. My father was on the front step of the trailer, and they were in a heated argument.

You must understand that, in our home, no one ever talked back to my father. Occasionally, he and my mother would fight, but mostly my father yelled. None of us children would dare talk back to him. Let alone raise our voices. The goal was usually to be as invisible as possible when we knew he was drunk, lest we trigger his ire. But here was my sister standing up to him, red-faced and screaming at him about how miserable he was and how much she hated him.

I was terrified, sure that it would result in someone getting terribly injured or killed, most likely my sister. Soon my mother shot past my father and screamed at him, trying to ensure he didn't escalate to physical violence. This was my worst nightmare. It would result in several things, all of which were bad. First, we were in unprecedented waters, with one of his children challenging him. I had no idea how this could ever de-escalate since I had only seen such things result in violence. And when it was over, where would my sister go now that she had challenged him? It had always been his house, his rules, even to my mom. Also, what would happen between him and mom now that she had joined the fray? Would she also be in danger? This would likely end up with my father drinking even heavier, and who knows what would result.

My sister had some sort of overnight bag in her hands that she moved to throw in the back seat of her car and slammed the door, as my mother kept my father distracted in an argument. Out of the corner of my eye, I saw a neighbor lady looking out her window and a man from the other side of my sister's car standing in the street, watching. Looking around, I noticed several other neighbors witnessing the incident. I could feel my face flushing with embarrassment. They must think we are a bunch of crazy red-necked hillbillies the way we were carrying on. I wanted to run and hide. My sister finally got in her car, yelling some more as she stood at the driver's door to get in her last words. I wondered where she would go as she sped away and out of the trailer park. Would I ever see her again, and what would happen here, now that my parents were arguing?

My father spun around and returned to the house, with my mother in close pursuit. I was hoping this would at least end the public spectacle. When I went inside to escape prying eyes and heads shaking in disgust, I had never seen my mother so mad. It wasn't much later that the police arrived, having been called by a neighbor. They threatened to take my father to jail but didn't since my sister was gone. The rest of the evening is lost in the endless parade of fights my parents would have every weekend when my dad was drunk. First, though, he took off in his car and came home hours later, even drunker than when he left.

The following Monday, my parents were notified that we had to move out because of the disturbance. We relocated to a larger trailer park about five miles away. This one was in Pennsville, the next town over, meaning we had to change schools. Ironically, it resulted in my brother and I attending the school a mile from where we used to live.

I don't remember my oldest sister ever living with us again. I think she went to my uncle's in Delaware, and I know she lived with my mom's parents in West Virginia for a while. She must have returned to the area at some point because she wrecked her car on the Delaware Memorial Bridge, which links southern New Jersey and Delaware. She was rear-ended when she stopped for a stalled car on the bridge, and I saw pictures of the mangled trunk of her car from the accident. A short time later, she married a man from Michigan, who was a pen pal, to escape my father because she had few options. That man would make her life miserable until she died of cancer in 2001. The best thing to come out of her marriage was my niece, Lisa, who would be nine years younger than me.

As a result of Ritzie moving out, the sleeping arrangement changed us. My brother had turned eight and complained about how crowded it was for us in the single bunk bed, while my youngest sister had the full-sized bed below us to herself. I tended to move around a lot in my sleep. It was common for me to wake up with my head at the foot of the bed by the morning, and my brother said I kicked a lot. My parents decided that the solution was to move me down to the full-size bed since I was the youngest so my brother could have his own bed. My sister wasn't thrilled with sleeping with a boy/mule who wandered and kicked, so each night, she constructed a wall of pillows between us.

If a leg or arm strayed on the wrong side of the pillows, a swift kick or punch soon woke me. My sister insisted on sleeping on the back of the bed where she had always slept, which put me on what I considered the front edge of the bed. So, I was inches from anyone walking down the hallway to the bathroom or my parents' room. When my father was drunk or my parents fought, I always tried to put my back against the pillows in the middle. I tried to get as far away from the edge as possible because he could just reach down and touch me. He had a habit of sitting on the foot of the bed and shaking me awake, even though I usually faked my slumber. When drinking, he needed an audience or would make us do something for him. Trying to ignore him only made him angry and he would soon find creative ways to get attention. This arrangement would be the source of nightmares throughout my teens and a definite source of my PTSD later.

Chapter 15

Two Women Fighting

The trailer park in Pennsville was much larger, probably three times the size of the one we had just left. Three small streets were perpendicular to the main road, each with three or four units. Behind these was a large loop that had approximately twenty units. We were at the back of the circle, fourth from the end. Our trailer faced away from the main road. Behind the trailer park were fields with woods around the edge. These were great for the many kids in the park to explore. I became friends with two boys a year or two younger who lived two trailers down from us. They were brothers named Gary and Glen, and their mother's name was Madeline. She was a blonde woman a little taller than my mom. On the other side of them was a family with a young girl a few years younger than Glen and Gary. Her name was Giselle, and her mom was Carlene, who became friendly with my mom. My parents said that Carlene was French and I thought it was exotic, like her daughter's name.

One of the boys had a birthday, and I was excited because I was invited to his party. I don't remember it being big, primarily the two brothers, me, and maybe one other boy from the neighborhood. His mother had made cupcakes and wisely had us eat them in the yard. It was a nice summer day, and we were happy to be outside. We were inside a small wire fence they had around the yard. Giselle came out of her house and asked if she could have a cupcake. We told her it was a birthday party and you had to be invited. I'm unsure if we teased her, but we weren't being nice and sharing. She started crying, and Madeline came out and explained that it was just for us boys at the birthday party. Giselle left crying and told her mom, who came over and spoke with Madeline. She then left, telling Giselle she would take her to the store and get a better cupcake.

We went on about our business of kids having a party, but I could tell that the boys' mom was upset from the encounter with Carlene. Giselle did reappear, remaining in her yard, clearly visible to us with a cupcake and ice cream her mother bought for her. I had assumed it had all blown over and thought no more about it.

A few days later in the evening, Madeline came over to our trailer looking for her boys for supper. I know it was evening because my dad was home, lying on the couch, watching TV. We were all in the house because we had just finished supper when she knocked on the door. My mother told her the boys weren't there. When Madeline turned to leave, she was confronted by Carlene, who started yelling obscenities about how her daughter had been treated and saying Giselle still cried about it. Madeline wanted nothing to do with her and tried to push past her, making the mistake of touching Carlene.

Carlene went after her, throwing slaps and fists, causing the two women to roll around on the sidewalk leading up to our steps. My mom tried to calm them down, and my brother and I slipped out past my mom to get a view of the fight. Mom advanced to the bottom of the steps and called for my dad. Out came my father, sober because it was a weekday, and he paused at the top of the steps.

This was my father, who had told us drunken stories of fights he had in bars back in West Virginia. He advised us that you get in trouble if you throw the first punch, so you had to feign like you were going to, and then when the other guy did, you fell on your back to raise up and kick him with both feet. My father was a World War II veteran of the Battle of the Bulge and Patton's third army. He had a purple heart and a bronze star for bravery. He was at least four inches taller than either of the women. This self-proclaimed tough guy stood at the top of the steps and yelled down, "You women shouldn't be doing that here. If you want to fight, go back to your own yards."

Meanwhile, Carlene had managed to rip Madeline's blouse off her. I was scared and excited because I had never seen a woman in a bra before, and I wanted to see more. I heard my brother yell, "Get her." I was sure he was also enjoying this. Carlene had her by the hair, pounding her head on the sidewalk, and then Madeline partially ripped Carlene's blouse. Just as it was getting good, my mom got them to separate, and Madeline lit for home at a run. Carlene stood there yelling at her, and my brother and I were taking in the sights. Madeline had scratches across her arms and chest and a black eye starting. Carlene had a few scrapes with her bra and cleavage showing. Her knuckles were skinned, and her hair was messy, but she still had some of Madeline's hair under her fingernails.

The cops came later, and my dad said he didn't know anything about it, and they were already on the ground when he looked out the door. He added that he wasn't about to get in between two crazy women and told them to go home. I felt terrible that somehow I was responsible since I hadn't offered to share my cupcake with Giselle but kept my mouth shut. Shortly after this incident, the family with the two boys moved. They had bought a house in a nicer part of Pennsville. Madeline would not let the boys come to our house because of the neighbors and my father's drinking. We said we'd keep in touch, and I went to visit and play once but never saw them after that.

Chapter 16

My First Bike

All the kids in the new neighborhood had bikes, and they rode them around constantly. I had gotten big for my trike but did not have a bicycle, so I was forced to chase them around on our scooter. For younger people, the scooters in the 1960s were similar to a razor, but they had six-inch wheels and tires and were about six inches wide. Needless to say, they were no match for a bicycle, and I was always lagging behind. Worse yet, I only had a wagon if the scooter was unavailable. Trying to catch a bike with one leg pushing a wagon while sitting in it was a very frustrating experience.

Buddy managed to get a bike. I don't remember if he got it when I received the scooter or if he assembled it from parts he acquired from his friends. My brother was much more mechanically inclined than I was at an early age. He blasted around with the other kids, no doubt embarrassed by his younger brother spastically chasing everyone in his wagon. I used to beg him to let me ride his bike, which he did occasionally, allowing me to perfect my two-wheeled skills.

I begged my mom for a bike to no avail. We weren't rich, and I'd have to wait until a birthday or Christmas came around. Several of those did pass with no bike forthcoming. It's not like we were totally neglected. We always had food, and a place to sleep, even if it was constantly interrupted sleep on the weekends. But my father had grown up during the depression and believed that money for toys was wasteful. It also cut into his drinking money. At least, that was what I believed.

Being only two years apart and living in the pressure cooker environment at home caused my brother and me to fight a lot. Buddy was always chubby when he was a kid. I was always skinny, so he was several inches taller and had me by probably thirty or more pounds. As a result, I lost most of the confrontations between us. But I had a temper that overruled this disadvantage and caused me not to shy from another butt-kicking. He hung around the older kids and ran me off when I followed him. I would complain to mom and get him in trouble when it suited me to get revenge. Eventually, I did make a few friends my age and became more independent.

One day my brother came to me and said he had a surprise. He took me outside, and there was a twenty-inch bike, the perfect size for me. He had pieced it together from parts he had scrounged from his friends or found tossed in a ditch or a junk pile. It wasn't the prettiest bike, but I loved it and rode it from morning until dark coming home only to eat lunch. I couldn't believe my brother had done this for me, and for a long time, I tried not to fight with him and to leave him alone with his friends. We would take baseball cards and put them on the fender brackets with clothes pins so that they were flipped by the spokes and would make a noise that sounded like a motorcycle engine. I had countless spills on the bike trying new skills and always came home with scrapes that my mom would cover with the dreaded mercurochrome. I would sit on the couch, knowing it would hurt, and move the injured limb as she approached it with the dropper.

"Hold still, you little baby," one of my siblings would inevitably say as they watched the process. My mom would blow on it, saying it would help, but it never did. All it would do was dry a bit faster. There were no helmets or gloves for kids back then, and we would have made fun of anyone who had the sense to wear them anyway. Being called a sissy was fighting words at that age and time. Speaking of that, I never had many fights as a kid except with my brother. If anyone older tried to bother me though, they would have to deal with my brother and older sister too. We may have had our internal battles, but we were also a protective unit if attacked from the outside.

Chapter 17

Visiting the Nurse

I managed to settle into the new school better than I expected. My new first-grade teacher was a nice older woman, and I liked her. I even had the honor of cleaning the chalkboard erasers for her allowing me to go out to the playground for a few minutes. I can remember standing outside on a breezy spring afternoon, the sun on my face. I would bang the erasers together and watch the chalk dust fly pretending they were tiny explosions. I did so well academically that the school approached my mom about having me skip the second grade. However, my oldest sister had skipped two grades, and my mother felt that it hurt her socially to be with the older kids, so she declined the offer. I didn't care because it let me progress along with the friends I had made.

I was worried about my mother at home throughout the first and second grades. After rough weekends of my parents fighting, or when my father came home drunk and raging, I would go to school exhausted and nervous, not recovered from the weekend. I remember sitting in the classroom and having trouble concentrating on what the teacher was saying. My thoughts would drift back to the battle over the weekend. Images of my father yelling and my mother screaming would fill my head. Worse yet, I would replay my father hitting my mom if the argument escalated to violence. It triggered images of her on the floor, bleeding or the black eye I had noticed as I kissed her goodbye that morning.

Even if he hadn't hit her, there were always threats made that haunted me. I imagined him going home from work at lunch, or leaving early, hitting her, possibly even killing her. I tried to imagine what life would be like without my mom. We would be trapped there alone with him, with no mother to protect us. He would treat us like slaves to wait on him. I knew nothing would please him, as I had witnessed constantly at home. He would come home drunk when we were all in bed. You could hear him singing loudly as he walked from the car. It would always be some Baptist hymn, usually about gathering at the river. He didn't sing because he was a happy drunk. It was done to wake us up, get attention, and make everyone focus on him.

He would come busting into the trailer, banging the door against the metal porch railing, and slamming it closed. Standing just inside the front door, looking down the hallway, he would shout something along the lines of, "Where's everybody? What's everybody doing in bed? You're old man's home. Ain't nobody gonna answer me?"

It could be ten o'clock at night or three in the morning. It didn't matter. This happened countless times in my life. It was one of the times of most danger. If you ignored him, he would just get increasingly angry and belligerent. He would not be ignored and would choose someone to harass. He often went into my parents' bedroom and stood over the foot of the bed near my mother.

"Shorty, you asleep?" kneeing the bed to shake it. Then he would find some reason for her to get up. He was hungry or wanted some coffee. Any excuse to get attention. If she ignored him, he would become more abusive.

"I didn't work all week to bring in food, to have you lay on your fat ass and sleep when your old man is hungry. You think that's right?"

My mom usually tried to ignore him, hoping he was so drunk that he would soon pass out. But most of the time, he would keep it up until she couldn't take it anymore and would come firing out of bed in full fury. I would be in my bed, straining to hear if there was any indication of a physical altercation that would result in my mom getting hurt. If I heard a slap, a crash, or any sign of violence, I would shoot out of bed, usually followed by my siblings to try to intervene.

My father's second scenario was to decide to bother one of us children, and as you may recall, the new sleeping arrangement had me on the front of the bottom bed. He would come into the bedroom and sort of huff standing there waiting for us to acknowledge him. He knew we had to be awake after his performance, but no one dared to break the illusion. I lay there with my pillow, usually over my head, but leaving just a tiny crack of the bottom lifted so I could see his legs to gauge his distance from me. As he stepped toward the bed, I would tense, unsure if he would sit on my legs or reach out and grab or touch me.

Interaction at this stage was never positive. It usually started with my father asking for or demanding something and descending into berating us or an endless string of tasks to entertain him by being waited on. Occasionally, my mom would come flying into the bedroom, telling him to leave the kids alone so we could rest for school tomorrow if it was Sunday. My brother was usually safest up in the bunk, with a wood railing in front. He seemed to like my brother more than me, so he seldom seemed to target him. My brother made an art of being invisible during my father's drunken rages. However, when he was older I remember several times he intervened to help protect my mom either by distracting or, less often, berating my father. But no one was totally safe.

This was how every weekend progressed in our home except for those blessed few when he came in and passed out on the bed, only to wake up Monday morning, puke his guts out, and then leave for work. These scenes passed through my head as I sat in class, wondering how my mother was doing or if he had gone home to carry out the threats he had made during his rants.

As I sat in class, trying to focus, these images came to the forefront. The visions of my mother on the floor, cut and bleeding, bruised and battered, repeated in my head like a horror movie. I would grow more anxious and begin hyperventilating, and tears would well in my eyes. I tried to hide it, but the teacher eventually noticed and asked what was wrong. I guess now it would be considered an anxiety attack. Still, with the class's attention suddenly focused on me, it was a struggle to keep from throwing up. I just wanted to hide or disappear. If pressed after first saying it was nothing, I would tell her my stomach hurt, I didn't feel well, and I had worked myself into such a state that it was true.

My first-grade teacher suggested that I go see the school nurse. The school districts had them at that time in each school. The teacher escorted me down to a small room near the principal's office. I was in an anteroom to the nurse's office, and she left me sitting on a chair to wait. I was terrified of being left alone, not knowing what would happen next, and growing concerned about my mother. When I heard the inner door open, a soft voice asked me what the trouble was. I was doubled over, staring at the linoleum-tiled floor with both arms wrapped around my stomach, trying not to puke. When I looked up, I saw the pretty blonde nurse in her twenties looking at me with a concerned look. I was speechless and smitten. She was the most beautiful woman I had ever seen. Even at the tender age of six, I was completely taken by this beauty, Ms. Sutton

After a few fits and starts, I squeaked out my stomach hurt. When she smiled at me, I felt a little better already. I didn't know what to expect next, but I was glad to be out of sight of the judging eyes of my classmates and telling her snapped me out of my reverie. I remembered my concern for my mother. The images flooded back, and a tear must have rolled down my cheek because she laid her hand on my face and gently wiped the tear away with her thumb, guiding me into her inner office. Ms. Sutton patted the chair seat, and I climbed into it. She closed her office door and sat at her desk, assuring me it would be okay. Then a miracle happened. She didn't grill me with questions about what I had eaten or probe me with tongue depressors or those long cotton-tipped Q-tip-looking things she had in jars on her cabinet. Instead, after consulting my file, she picked up the phone and called my mom. I heard her talk briefly to my mom, then turn to me.

"Your mom is coming to pick you up," she smiled at me again, and I instantly felt better.

That meant my mom was alive and okay enough to come and get me. What a relief. Most of my anxiety left me in that instant. I didn't know what to do. Should I tell her I felt better? Would I get in trouble? I had set things into motion now that were bigger than me. I had left class and involved the nurse. My mom would have to find a ride because she didn't have her own car, and my dad was at work. I couldn't just say never mind. Oh, I was in big trouble for sure. I would have to ride it out, though. That bridge had been crossed.

The nurse took me into a separate little room where they had a bed and told me to lie down until my mom arrived. I would much rather have sat staring at her, but the ball was in motion now, so I dutifully laid down. In the room alone, some anxiety returned, less for my mom and more regarding how I could maintain this charade. It took my mom a while, and the nurse checked in on me. She caught me staring at the stuff in the cabinet, with my foot anxiously twitching back and forth. I told her I felt a little better, and she told me to rest.

Finally, my mom came, and I immediately felt guilty when I saw the look of concern on her face. She had gotten a ride from a neighbor, and I could tell she felt embarrassed at having to come to school and beg for a ride from anyone. I thanked the nurse and melted again as she smiled and touched my head. In the car, I was subject to a barrage of questions by both my mom and the neighbor. I thought I managed to answer them adequately. Fortunately, the neighbor was a loquacious woman who soon began talking with my mom, turning the focus away from me. I sat in the back, looking out the window, feeling outside of my existence because I was not where I was supposed to be. I was in a strange car. My mother was close, and I felt safe, but it was almost like watching the world from someone else's point of view. I had stepped out of the frightening world where I lived into a possible world where mom could hang out with friends, go places with them, and we would both be safe. I wanted to stay there.

Back at the trailer court, we walked from the neighbors to our trailer. Each step that we took brought that world of fear and violence closer. When she opened the door, and we entered, I didn't feel at home, but like I had been dragged back into a darker world. My stomach churning returned, and I went and laid down with my pillow over my head. That was the first day I promised myself it would be different someday. I would leave and build a world where I would feel safe and control who was in my life.

Eventually, my brother and sister came home, running into the house to tell my mom I wasn't on the bus. It was actually nice to see that they were concerned for me. My brother called me a little baby when my mom told them I hadn't felt well. My sister admonished me for not telling them I was home already. I didn't know how I would have done that. The crisis was averted. They both got changed and went about their regular after-school routines. No one said anything to my father, and I was grateful, as he would have just said I was just seeking attention.

It wasn't the last time I saw Miss Sutton. Whenever I saw her in the hallway, I would always say hello, and a few times, I thanked her again for helping me. She remembered my name and always smiled, tousling my blonde hair. I went to that school through third grade and ended up at her office probably two other times on a Monday after a rough weekend at home. Again, I was sent home, but they became less frequent as I matured and developed more coping mechanisms.

Chapter 18

Yet Another Move

I sat at the table during the summer after third grade as my mother worked in the kitchen. She was likely making a peanut butter and jelly sandwich for my lunch since I lived on them during those years.

"Mom, I don't know if I'm ready for fourth grade."

"Why not?" she turned to look over her shoulder, surprised. I had done well in third grade.

I spun my glass of Kool-Aid on the table, pondering if I should tell her, but I had painted myself into a corner now. "Well, in first through third grades, when we go out for recess, we all play together as a class, and we have a fifth grader who helps and acts as a recess monitor."

"Okay, well, what's the problem?"

"For the fourth and fifth graders, they just turn them loose on the playground in the back, so they can play a pick-up baseball game or whatever they want. They all played together! Those fifth graders are pretty big! I don't know if I'm ready for that." I was sure a skinny little kid like me would be picked on, and my brother would be no help because he would be transferred to the middle school on the other side of town for sixth grade.

"Well, you'll do some growing this summer. Why don't we wait to see how you feel in September." She stood looking at me to judge my reaction.

"Okay," I answered, but I couldn't imagine how I could grow enough. I had been stuck at around forty pounds since last Christmas.

It turned out that the playground arrangements would be the least of my worries. Shortly after that conversation, my father got into a confrontation with some neighbors across the lane. I don't remember what started it. The neighbor may have driven too fast when we were out playing, but it happened during the weekend, and my father was drunk. I can barely remember some threats of an ass-kicking and possibly mention of a gun was made. My mom screamed at him, trying to drag him back to our side and into the trailer. Before long, the police came, and it was the first time I remember my father being loaded into the back of a police car. We received notice to move before the end of the week.

All of us kids cried the day of the move, not wanting to change schools again and lose touch with our friends. The new place was way out on the other side of the next township amid farm country and was another small trailer park. That meant fewer kids and a new school, making us miserable initially. I hated my father for his drinking and fighting. I was sure it was just a matter of time before he'd get us kicked out of this one.

The trailer beside us had a family with two kids, but they were both too young for me to play with. One boy lived up the street with his grandparents a year or so younger than me, and the owner of the park had two kids, but they were girls. The only other family with kids were relatives of the owner, but the boy was too young also. I played with the kid who lived with his grandparents. Still, we had wildly different personalities, and it wasn't too long until he left, I assume to go back to his mom. In short, this place sucked, other than plenty of woods around.

I spent a miserable month riding my bike in circles around the park, and then it was time for school to start. The week before, they published the class assignments in the local paper. To my horror, I discovered that my fourth-grade teacher would be a man. I never had a male teacher. My previous elementary schools had no male teachers, and I was terrified. Would he yell at us like my father did or hit the kids? I had no idea what to expect from him, but I was sure he wouldn't like me.

On the first day of class, he introduced himself to me since he knew most other students in the school from previous years. Mr. Sorrels even introduced me to the class, which I found humiliating. Who wants to be the new kid? He had a soft speaking voice but was also animated at times, probably to keep us interested. Still, any change in voice or behavior had me on the edge of tears because I was sure it indicated him starting to go off on a rant. A week or so into the school year, after another tumultuous weekend, I had a meltdown in class and asked to see the nurse. I tried to hide my tears, but he managed to see through the façade. He took me into the hallway to talk to me and put his hand on my shoulder, speaking in a soft, concerned voice. I jumped at his touch, causing him to look even more curious, but he did escort me to the nurse's office.

The protocol at this school district was different than Ms. Sutton's. The nurse was more middle-aged, and she first sat me down and put a thermometer in my mouth. I asked her if she would call my mom, but she said nobody goes home unless they have a fever. My heart stopped. I was trapped, afraid to return to class, and unable to go home. What would they do with me? When she returned to remove the thermometer, tears were streaming down my face, though I had managed to stifle any sobs. She disappeared down the hallway. I would later find she went to talk to Mr. Sorrels to determine what happened to me. When she returned, she had me lie down in a separate room and try to relax a little, assuring me that everything would be okay.

Since I was worried about my mom, I asked if I could call her. I didn't say it was to make sure she was okay. The nurse said she would talk to her. I heard her on the phone, and I can only assume that my mom must have told her about our home life because the nurse was on the phone for a while then returned and told me I could lie there as long as needed. She must have also informed Mr. Sorrels. After a while, I calmed down since the nurse talking to my mom meant she wasn't dead or hurt. I started getting bored and told the nurse I thought I could return now. When I got there, Mr. Sorrels came back into the hallway and told me not to worry, and whenever I didn't feel up to class, I could lie down at the nurse's office. He was very kind, and I felt bad for being scared of him earlier, but I had seen my dad be nice at times, too, so I was still a bit wary. I was surprised when Mr. Sorrels called my mom after school to ask about what happened and discuss our home life. I wasn't sure if that meant I was in trouble, but he seemed to give me a little extra attention afterward.

The recesses I had worried about at the other school were a mix of open forums and some organized sports. Mr. Sorrels organized some of the softball games. I played some since baseball and softball were my best sports, though I was no star. I was pretty good at fielding but had never batted at a pitched ball since we mostly played what we called pop-up or hit the bat at home because we didn't have enough kids to field a team. As a result, my batting sucked. He must have noticed that I always borrowed someone else's glove because he pulled me aside one day after the other kids had run out the door for recess. I wasn't sure what to expect, but he pulled out a baseball glove that was a color I had never seen. I was used to the cowhide tan-colored glove, and this one was almost a dark brownish/purple. He told me it was his glove when he was a kid, and it was a first baseman's glove. It was unlike the modern ones I had seen because instead of having one open side where you could put all your fingers, this one had four. He saw my confusion and showed me how to wear it. It had a special hole on the back that let you put your index finger out behind the mitt to give it more protection from fast throws from infielders. I didn't know what to say. It was obviously very special to him.

"You mean I can use it today? Thanks!"

"No. I'm giving it to you. It's a special glove I have cared for since I was your age, and I want you to have it."

"Really?"

"Yes. And I hope it serves you as well as it did me."

"Oh my gosh. I love it. Thanks!"

I took it out with me and ran to play softball. I was so worried that I might hurt it. I did get a few strange looks and comments like, "What is that?" I'd proudly tell them it was a first baseman's glove, was real, and probably way older than them. I took care of that glove until I left home, when I forgot to grab it, losing it in the move. I still regret losing it. Whenever I would field a ball for the rest of the year, I would look over, and Mr. Sorrels winked at me. He was my favorite teacher after that. Not only did he give me a gift, but he trusted me with something special. In that class, I began to promise myself to go to college. I might be a teacher or not, but I would be an educated man like Mr. Sorrels.

He also started another habit for me. In the fall, he handed out a catalog of books we could order. They were kids' novels and other books that we could read. All were paperback, and most were about three dollars. I looked through the catalog and found some I thought I would like. I pleaded with my mom, who managed to scrape together enough change for me to order something. Mr. Sorrels sent away the order, and it seemed like forever, so much so that I almost forgot, but finally, a box arrived. The excitement was palpable in the room as he opened the box and read the list of who ordered what as he handed them out. That excitement has stayed with me my whole life. Mr. Sorrels gave me my love of reading, which has served me well over the years. I still feel it as I open a new book and begin reading it.

Once school started, my brother and I made an important discovery. A family just down the road lived on what the father called a gentleman's farm with three boys around our age. By gentleman farmer, he meant he worked outside the home instead of making his living farming. That family was the Jennings family, and I met the brothers on the school bus. There was Johnny, who was the same age as my brother, Stanley, who was between Buddy and me, and Jerry, who was two years younger. There was also a girl about my youngest sister's age and another near my age. The boys all had a muscular build compared to my chubby brother's build and my skinny one and they seemed to be a bit of a rough crowd. Their farm was a quarter mile away via the road, so we didn't visit much initially since we were told to stay off of the road.

At this point, I would have been around eight. Once we knew the family better, my brother started hanging around Stanley, who went by the nickname of "Sug," short for Sugarfoot, his favorite TV show. I paired up with Jerry, who was given the nickname Hawkeye by his father, which was eventually shortened to "Hawky." It wasn't long before we were inseparable, though the older boys never wanted us hanging around, but we copied them in their activities. If they built a tree fort, we would also. A few years later, when they started a log cabin, so did we. We completed ours, including a fifty-gallon barrel for a stove. However, we could never use it because its residual oil smoked us out of the cabin. As we got older and more confident, we settled into a routine that made living out in the country more fun, and we didn't miss our friends from the other trailer park so much.

Chapter 19

Jehovah's Witnesses

It was a summer day on a Saturday. Late morning, I had already eaten breakfast. I was ready to disappear for the day before my father could get too far along on his drinking. As I jumped on my bike and started to tear across the yard, the chain slipped and came off the sprockets. Crap! I pushed the bike back to the patio and flipped it over to see what was happening. It was a third-hand stingray style that was popular back then, but mine had been cobbled together using a mixture of parts. I saw that the nuts on the back axle had loosened from the recent jumps we had been doing. Hawky and I had built a ramp out of a small dirt hill, competing to see who could go the greatest distance in the air.

I needed wrenches, which meant a further delay in disappearing. It also increased the risk of my father catching me and making me do something so he could boss someone around and feel important. Double crap! I ran to the shed and grabbed a Cresent wrench and a box-end that would fit. Hurrying back to the bike, I pulled the wheel back, so the chain was now taut and tightened the nuts. Spinning the pedals, I tested it, and all seemed good. Great. I ran to the shed and put the wrenches back, then jogged to my bike and was just about to turn it back onto its wheels when I saw two men starting up our sidewalk. They were well-dressed in white shirts and ties. One man had a hat cocked smartly on his head like I saw detectives wear in the old movies. Both were carrying bibles, and one seemed to have some kind of brochures in his other hand.

Huh, this is unusual, I thought as they approached. Several houses of black people lived about a half-mile up the road in what my parents called the colored section. However, all the people in the park were white, and I had never seen black people visit. Our school was probably forty percent black kids, some of whom I thought of as friends, although I didn't know them as well as my white friends. I assumed the men were interested in discussing church since they carried Bibles.

As we made eye contact, I smiled and started to say hello, but was interrupted by my father charging out of the front door. He stopped atop the steps, and with his hands on his hips, he practically yelled, "What the hell do YOU want?"

The men stopped, and all eyes swung to my father. The man without the hat held out his Bible for my father to see, answering, "We wanted to talk to you about Jesus Christ, sir. Do you know our Lord and Savior?" He smiled as he waited for the answer.

"You're not one of them Martin Luther King niggers are you?" That phrase will be forever burned in my memory. I was stunned. Standing there with my chin practically down to my knees, I didn't know what to feel most. I was terrified by what could happen next. Would it escalate to a fight or my father threatening them with a gun? I was humiliated by what he had said. I wanted to be as far away as possible and to scream at my father about what an asshole he was. I wanted to somehow comfort those poor men after such an unprovoked attack.

Seconds passed as the men tried to recover and collect themselves. The man in the hat reached out and gently tugged on the other man's elbow, trying to guide him off our property, his jaw set hard and his eyes burning at my father. The touch seemed to snap the hatless man out of his shock. He gave my father a stiff smile and said, "You have yourself a nice day, sir. We'll pray for you and your family." They turned and walked out of the yard.

My father stood there glaring at them, ensuring they didn't return. He turned to go back inside, looking back one last time for good measure. I watched him go back inside, flipped my bike back to its wheels, jumped on it, and exited. I raced through the path in the woods that led to the road, playing back the episode in my head, becoming increasingly disgusted. Even then, it occurred to me that I was awfully young to lose total respect for my father. I was at the age where you were supposed to tell the other kids that your dad could beat up theirs.

I was a kid who knew my parents did not like black people. They were also referred to pejoratively. I had been indoctrinated all my life. I always assumed they had their reasons, some bad interaction from the past. They had made comments behind closed doors, where expressing opinions is safe. But being so blatant, aggressive, and seemingly ignorant caused another wave of embarrassment to roll over me like a chill.

I didn't slow down until halfway to my friend Hawky's house. The embarrassment flowed so profoundly that I didn't even mention the encounter to my friend when I arrived at his house, preferring to try to forget it.

Chapter 20

Introduction to a Life-long Addiction

I had been after my parents for years, telling them I wanted a new bicycle. I was tired of seeing other kids in school come cruising up on the latest trendy bicycles they had received for birthdays or Christmas. One advantage of living so far out of town was that my school friends did not ever see the scrap heap refugee I was forced to ride. My friend Hawky was the only one, and he was in the same boat, being the youngest boy with three older brothers. His bike was also a hand-me-down configuration of parts from his older brothers' rejects.

We made the best of it that we could. At one point, both of us had bikes with multi-speed rear rims. Hawky had a three-speed sting ray, and I had a five-speed rear rim that I had found somewhere. Finding the shifter, and especially a cable that would work with my bike, had been a struggle, but we had both finally done it. Neither of us could afford the components for the rim-style hand-activated brakes needed for multi-speed bikes, so we rode without brakes. To compensate for no brakes, there were two ways of stopping. We would stop pedaling but keep our feet on the pedals. Then when we needed to stop, lean back and throw the back wheel out sideways so that we were perpendicular to whatever we were trying to avoid. This also had the added benefit of leaving an excellent skid mark in the dirt where the back wheel slid. This worked well off-road and at relatively slow speeds. On either blacktop or concrete pavement, you ran the risk of putting too much weight on the back tire. This would cause it to gain too much traction, causing a "high side," which pitched you face-first into the hard surface.

The second method of stopping simply involved sticking your foot in the front forks, using the bottom of your foot as a brake against the tire's surface. Our bikes never had fenders. This worked really well, with two drawbacks. The first was that if you wore a shoe, usually a sneaker, it would quickly wear a groove the width of the tire into the bottom of your shoe. While this was the one time that I was glad that I was forced to wear the $1.99 sneakers from Acme (the grocery store) instead of the cool and highly desired Converse sneakers or even Keds. However, if I went through my sneakers too quickly, there would be hell to pay, or I wouldn't get a new pair. Sneakers were supposed to last a year in our world.

The second drawback to this braking method happened if you were barefoot, which was most of the summer for both Hawky and me. You could easily burn the bottom of your foot with just one emergency stop. It only took one time to figure out this disadvantage was to be avoided. However, that did not prevent Hawky and me from playing our favorite game on the bikes besides pulling wheel stands or jumping. Since neither of us had brakes, the logical thing to do was to see who could follow the other the closest and not crash. So one bike would go in front, and the other person would put their front tire as close to the back tire of the first bike and keep it there as long as possible. The object of the front bike was to make this as hard as possible for the other guy by changing speed and/or direction, jumping things, or anything else that would make this difficult. Hours of entertainment would follow. The need for brakes and the coolness factor were why I always hinted at a new bike.

Since Buddy got along with my father much better than I did, he occasionally went with him on weekends. I remember one such time that they had gone somewhere in my dad's truck, which I gave little thought to at the time. I was inside when they came home, and my father announced that he had a surprise. We went out to his truck, and he and my brother were unloading a Honda 50cc Passport motorcycle. My father had bought it from my Uncle Dick for $100. I was pissed off because he could have both of us brand new stingrays for that money.

I also didn't like the looks of Passport because of its design. It was a step-through design like a girl's bicycle. The gas tank was under the seat instead of in front of the seat. It also had a little shield in front of your legs. An automatic/centrifugal clutch completed the package. To me, it screamed, "girl's bike." In the early sixties, Honda tried to change the public perception of people who ride motorcycles with their "You meet the nicest people on a Honda" campaign. So, this was designed to look more like the Italian scooters people were used to seeing.

Reluctantly I took my first test ride after brief instruction from my brother. As part of my revenge for talking my father into it, I tried it so my brother would not get to ride it all the time. I was hooked. It went faster than a bicycle and was a blast to ride. Buddy and I rode it constantly, taking turns until the engine case was warm enough we were afraid it would overheat. We need not worry because the little Honda would prove almost indestructible over the next few years. We started riding a path in the woods about a quarter mile long, then had a circular turnaround and returned. It was traveled so much that in the summer months, it would be packed hard enough you could lock the back wheel and the tire would squeal on the dirt.

Soon we explored everywhere, even on short excursions on the road to get to our friend's house down the street. Sug had a motorcycle, a ninety cubic centimeter Honda, so he and my brother cruised around exploring roads, woods, and fields. We fought over it so much that my father eventually found a 1956 two-stroke Zundapp 250 that looked like an antique tank compared to the modern bikes. It had massive fenders, and the styling looked like World War II surplus, but it was fast. That became Buddy's because he was stronger and bigger since it weighed a ton compared to the little Honda. I was happy with the Honda and rode it everywhere. The bicycles were relegated to when we went somewhere on the roads where the police could be. Hawky never had a motorcycle, but he had a mini-bike temporarily, so he usually rode with me. Our adventures on the motorcycles could fill a book by themselves. Still, it started a life-long hobby/obsession that continues today.

Chapter 21
Sleeping in the Field

My mother began standing up for herself and intervening when my father started picking on the three of us children. I am not sure what started it. Perhaps it was thinking back on how badly my father had treated my oldest sister Ritzie (Rita). It could also have been influenced by increased support from the community we now lived in or that she got tired of his antics. She had always argued with him for as long as I could remember, but she also began to confront him more. Of course, this had the effect of increasing the number of escalations to violence at times. It also made me worry for her since it meant she had more chance of getting hurt.

When things did escalate, there were two most likely outcomes for the argument because very rarely did my father walk away once he went on a rant. If my mother stood her ground, it would likely end in him hitting her, with all three of us children standing around screaming and crying. Once he did that, he would either take off in his car, perhaps out of guilt or to avoid getting arrested. Occasionally, it did end up with the police being called. Of course, anytime that happened, we ran the risk of being forced to move again. Several times we were given notice, but because we kids had gotten close to the owner's family, riding to church with them, they rescinded the order several times. I will always be grateful for the stability they gave us.

Also likely would be my mother saying we were leaving. She would gather us and go to a neighbor's or relative's house. Ritzie had moved back from Detroit, and for a while, she, her husband, and her daughter lived in the same trailer park. Her husband was six foot or so and weighed a good three hundred pounds, so my father was not likely to follow us there.

Other times my mom would grab a bunch of blankets and pillows and head out to the woods, where we would spread them out and sleep on the ground. If it were summer, it might only be for a few hours. She would stay awake and watch until things settled in the trailer, and my father eventually passed out. We would sneak back into the trailer, and she would spend the rest of the night on the couch. The following day my father would wake up and throw up, then get dressed and go to work if it was Monday. Monday night, a stressful silence would descend on the world, or my mother would say a few sharp words while my father lay on the couch watching television.

The rule of the house was that we had to be inside when the streetlights came on. My brother and I would play within sight of the house as it began to get dark, trying to determine how safe it was and maximize our time before entering. Once you entered at dark, you were trapped for the duration. One memorable Sunday, my father's car was not home, so we knew it would be safe at least to enter. Once in, if he did not make it for dinner, you would spend the evening dreading when he did show. Since the food was ready, we ate as quickly as possible so we wouldn't be caught at the table with him. Then we would scatter as much as we could within a ten-by-fifty-foot trailer. This particular night he finally showed up around 9:30, and the first clue to his degree of intoxication was we could hear him singing "Shall We Gather at the River" as loud as he could. This would not be a good night unless we got lucky, and he passed out.

The table was cleared hours ago, and the dishes were washed, which increased the likelihood of an outburst from him. However, my mom had decided to stand her ground about him not showing up for dinner. He stomped up the steps, threw the door open so it would hit the metal railing with a bang, then stumbled into the doorway. Looking around with blinking, unfocused eyes, he took us all in. My mom was in the recliner in the corner of the living room, her usual spot. I was beside her, squatted on the heater vent beside her chair, which was both a warm and protected spot. My sister and brother were both at the table, Annette doing her homework, and Buddy watching Bonanza on the TV with my mother and me. It was a cold night, and the frigid air flowed In, announcing a drop in the mood.

"Close the damned door," my mother told him. He glared at her briefly before turning and slamming it shut.

"Where's my goddamned supper?" he barked, weaving in place and eyeing the empty head of the table where he always sat. Oh crap. Not a good start. My mother ignored him, pretending to watch the show. My brother slipped from the table into our bedroom, and my sister began putting her books away.

"Why ain't there no goddamned supper on the table?" More silence. "You too goddamned lazy to get off your fat ass and make supper?" She still held back, ignoring him. "You think I work all week to buy the goddamned groceries so you can sit on your fat ass while I go hungry?" He took a step forward, his knee hitting the arm of the couch, and he used it to steady himself, though his upper body still wavered as he tried to focus on the target of his anger. His fists were clenched, and his face flushed as usual when drinking, giving him a satanic appearance, a demon incarnate. I felt a shiver go through me as I sat in the stream of forced hot air from the vent.

"The kids ate supper when we always do. Not my fault you

didn't bother to show up. Yours is in the refrigerator if you want it," my mom said slowly and deliberately, with amazing coolness.

"You ain't gonna fix me something to eat?" His fists clenched then unclenched as he awaited the answer, which failed to come. Seeing he was ignored, he took a different tact. I sat staring with all my might at the television screen, trying to pretend this was not happening. In my peripheral vision, I saw his eyes shift to me.

"Mike." His hillbilly accent grew exaggerated when drunk so that it came out sounding more like Mack. "How 'bout you fix your old man something to eat since your damned mother is too lazy to do it." He knew that redirecting his attack on one of the kids would elicit a response from my mom.

She was out of the chair like a lightning bolt, standing before him with her finger in his face, yelling, "You son of a bitch, don't you go saying I didn't do my job. I had supper on the table when it was supposed to be. It's not my fault you were out whoring around 'til all hours, and you missed it." She moved so fast that he leaned away from her as he tried to focus on the fury before him.

She stormed to the refrigerator, opened it, pulled out a plate covered with cellophane, and tossed it on the table. Pivoting, she opened the silverware drawer and tossed a fork, spoon, and knife, so they slid next to the plate announcing, "There's your goddamned supper." Then she stormed into the back bedroom, leaving him weaving in her wake.

"Huh," he said, then sat at his place. He took a bite of something on his plate, but I knew he wouldn't eat. He wasn't hungry. It was all a show. After pushing things around on his plate, he stood up and looked around. I ducked behind the table on my right, trying to be as small as possible. Since he was seated at the table, he didn't turn around. I don't think I was in view, and my sister had already changed and gotten in bed. There was no one for him to mess with.

He stood up and staggered back through to my parent's bedroom. Like my sister, my mom had already changed and was in bed. He stopped at the foot of the bed, standing over her. Her side of the bed was against a wall, so it was inaccessible to him. Instead, he bumped the bed with his knee.

"Shorty, I know you're not asleep, goddamn it." She ignored him again, so I could hear him bump the bed harder as it thudded against the wall. I was in a precarious position being the only one not in bed. If he came back here, I would be obvious, but if I tried to get to the bedroom, he would see me in the hallway. I crept out far enough to see the edge of his shoulder. He walked around the end of the bed to where he was out of sight. Using this opportunity, I slunk into the bedroom and bed without changing my clothes.

I took up my usual defensive position with my back against the wall of pillows to be as far away from the edge as possible, covers up to my ears. My pillow was over my head with enough of a crack underneath that I could see his legs if he entered our bedroom. My pillow was thin enough to hear some of what was happening in the back bedroom. I could hear him talking, then he came lumbering back down the hallway and stood in the doorway between the bathroom and our bedroom. I could see his legs wobbling unsteadily as he decided on his next assault. Finally, he slammed the sliding bathroom door so hard that it bounced back partially open, allowing him to do it again. He knew it would wake us up if we were asleep.

Of all the things we didn't need, I heard him make himself another drink. Then he cleared his throat loudly, and I heard him stomp back into the other bedroom with a new initiative. With the near door closed, I could only hear muffled voices, both his and my mom's, then a loud thud. I went on high alert, sitting on the edge of the bed, straining to hear. He said something, and my mom's voice responded in a raised tone. Things were escalating. I had cracked the bathroom door when I heard my mom's feet hit the floor and saw her standing at the foot of their bed.

"I told you to leave me alone, you bastard, and I mean it." Her chin was jutted out, and I could tell she was angry now. He came around the bed, and she put both hands on his chest and pushed him as hard as she could into his secretaries' desk on their back dresser. He rolled off onto the floor, struggling to get to his feet.

Annette and I were yelling for them to stop and for my father to leave her alone. Finally reaching his feet, he pointed at her and said, "Did you see what that bitch just did to me? That's assault, and I have a right to defend myself." He advanced toward her with his right arm cocked to throw a punch.

My sister shot past me. "Dad, come on now. You've had a drink or two. If somebody calls the cops, who do you think will go to jail?" This distracted him long enough that my mom walked into the bathroom and began pulling on some slacks under her nightgown.

"Kids, get dressed." She looked at me funny because I still had on my clothes. "We can't stay here tonight. He's too drunk."

She stopped by our closet, pulled out the spare blankets and quilts, handed one to each of us, and then grabbed pillows off our bed. My brother, sister and I quickly dressed, grabbing our heaviest coats. As we did, my father came charging forward to the bathroom doorway.

"Where the fuck do you think you're going? It's below freezing out there." He stood with his hands on his hips, sneering at us. "You whoring around with old man Henry or one of the niggers up the road?" Mr. Henry was an older gentleman who lived in the neighborhood alone, which is why he was mentioned.

My mom stopped in her tracks for a second and spun to face him. He had achieved his goal of goading her. "I'd be better off with one of them niggers, than living here with you." Then she spun back around and herded us out of the trailer.

As the first one out the door, the crisp air stunned my face as if I had been slapped. Digging into my coat pockets, I pulled out the gloves and knit cap I had stuffed there. Putting them on and standing up my collar, I tried to disappear into the coat so that I was just peeking out over the top of the fake shearling collar.

My sister behind me said, "Are you sure about this, mom?"

"Yes." My mother had been bullied, insulted, her integrity

attacked, sleep interrupted, and possibly assaulted. I saw a look of determination in her eyes that would not let her turn back.

At that, I dropped back and followed my mother as she led us toward the front of the trailer court. She was looking for a place he wouldn't find us, with a space ample enough for us to make a bed.

I thought of my tree fort near the entrance. "We could take turns sleeping in my tree fort, but we wouldn't all fit," I suggested. Mom seemed to consider it and walked over to where she could judge the size of it but decided against the option since it was only large enough for three if we really packed in.

Across the main road was a clearing in the woods where a house had been years ago. The only thing that remained was part of the foundation, and further back was the tin roof of a collapsed outbuilding that I had been told was once a pig pen. We crossed the road, trudging through knee-high weeds that crunched in the cold and glistened in the light of a near-full moon, showing a dusting of frost already formed on them. She found a spot underneath two tall pear trees near their life's end. What few branches there were, were misshapen like the disfigured arms of goblins in the moon's reflection. I worried that I might not be able to get to sleep as they stood over me in the dark.

We had three quilts, one blanket, and four pillows. My mom began stomping the weeds and spreading a quilt and blanket on the ground. I tried to assist but kept getting distracted, looking around for my father or other wild animals that could be a threat. She tossed the pillows down, pulling one from my arms, startling me as I stared up at the goblins again.

"Lay down," she commanded.

We all looked at her and then at each other, waiting to see who would go first. Finally, my brother lay on the side farthest from the road. I laid down some distance from him, knowing he would complain if I were close. As she spread the first of two heavy quilts, my sister laid down on the other edge because that was where her pillow had been placed. Once she spread the second quilt, my mother crawled between my brother and me. The weeds beneath the bottom quilt sounded like the crackle of a fire in the frigid night air whenever someone moved.

I lay there shivering beneath the still-cold blankets staring up at the sky as I peeked out between my knit cap and the collar, blankets pulled above my chin. I gazed up at the indigo sky, silver moonlight bathing the southern side of the goblins, occasional gusts making their arms reach toward me. I doubted I could ever get to sleep.

"Look! Shooting stars," my brother said. He thrust a gloved hand skyward.

"Where?" my sister and I said in chorus. I had never seen a shooting star and desperately searched the winter sky, finally daring to look past the scary trees. The ground seemed to move beneath me as the sky suddenly enveloped us. There were so many stars, and I lay breathless as I tried to take them in. Eyes adjusting to the distance, I thought I saw movement to my right periphery.

"Look, another one," my sister said. I wasn't sure if I had genuinely seen it or if my eye movement was causing the effect because I wasn't looking directly at it. Goblins now forgotten, my focus was to catch the next one as I scanned the sky. I lay listening to the crackle of the dried plants beneath us as we breathed and shifted. I felt a collective warmth finally gathering beneath the blankets, luring me to sleep. I tried to stay awake to witness this miracle of the heavens others in their warm beds would never see. I felt safe between my mom and sister, much more than I did at home. I wondered if we could always sleep here. I wondered how to take a shooting star to class for show and tell. I must focus and stay awake.

The next thing I knew, it was morning. Mom was trying to wake us even though the light was still pink as the sun had just begun its battle with the chilly temperatures. I saw a thick layer of frost on the top quilt as I sat up. Scraping at it with my gloved finger, I flicked it at my sister, who was stiffly trying to stand.

We walked back through the trailer park, still silent in the early hour, my mom and I sharing a quilt wrapped around us. Back at the trailer, we snuck in, trying not to wake my unconscious father, going to bed fully clothed, wanting just to get in a warm bed. My mother wrapped the quilt around her and lay on the couch to catch an hour's sleep before my father's alarm went off for work.

All of us would go to school red-eyed and tired, doing our best to act as if we were a normal family. We had survived another weekend.

Chapter 22
Nicknames

Growing up, I longed to have a real nickname. Some could argue that Mike was a nickname for Michael, but let's be honest. It is just people being lazy and truncating the name on my birth certificate. I was surrounded by people with nicknames. Instead of Ernest, my father was called Red. My brother was Ernest Junior (thank God I was second), and everyone called him Buddy. Rita was Ritzie which is both longer and has a second meaning, so according to my rules, qualifies. My youngest sister's real first name was Patricia, but we all called her Annette, her middle name.

All of the Jennings boys had nicknames, even some of the girls. Stanley was Sug, Jerry was Hawkeye, and Johnny was called Murphy for some reason. Their youngest sister Joan we called Bulldog, though she hated it. They were all characters, including their dad, who usually assigned nicknames and told stories about how tough the Japanese soldiers were in World War II. He talked about how they could hold up for years in the mountains living on fish heads and rice.

I wondered if my lack of a nickname meant I had no personality or if people did not like me enough to give me a cool nickname. I tried to think up a cool one for myself but discovered that nicknames don't seem to work if you tried to convince others it was your new identity. I asked my mom how my other sibling came to have them, and I didn't. To my surprise, they were much more logical than I had assumed and had nothing to do with personality. My oldest sister's nickname was a variation of her name that they called her as a baby that stuck. My youngest sister's first name was picked by my father, and it was an old girlfriend's name, so my mother called my sister by her middle name, chosen by my mom. Neither parent liked Ernest Arthur Junior, so they started calling him their little buddy. It was my mom's turn to name me, and since she liked Michael, I was always just called Mike. Except by the Jennings.

The Jennings family also had some older kids that were grown, so they weren't part of my world. They had a daughter Mary who I only saw a few times, and a son, Michael or Mike, who joined the Marines during Viet Nam soon after I began hanging around with them. He was later killed when a land mine exploded as he was instructing someone on how to disarm it. In their eyes, he became almost a mythic hero, so I could never be called Mike because that was his name. They all called me Mikepatton. I write it here without space because they all said it very fast, almost like one syllable. It was always "Hey, Mikepatton. How are you?" Even my friend Hawky in all the time we hung around together, if he wanted my attention, it was "Mikepatton, look."

I guess I should be grateful since they are typically assigned by others. Glad I didn't end up with a nickname like "stinker," which was my youngest sister's nickname until she went to grade school. I could have been four-eyes when I started wearing glasses in eighth grade. My siblings did try to torment me as a kid, especially given the temper I had not learned to control yet. I won't go into those, as they were taunts, not nicknames. I had mine for them too. But if nicknames are supposed to indicate some strong personality trait, I guess I never had one. I spent most of my time trying to appear normal.

Being of average height and a thin build, I couldn't be "Stretch" or "Chubby." That was okay with me. I'm still unsure how I escaped it, though, for later in life, my brother seemed to nickname everyone he met. All of his kids, friends, and many of his co-workers. It must have been my mom's fondness for my given name.

Chapter 23
Throwing the Plate

Violence in our world often resulted from an argument that escalated the entire weekend. It would build, ebbing and flowing, so your nerves frayed, expecting it to explode any second until you entered a time warp of never-ending tension. It could also catch you off guard, flaring up in a heartbeat. The front wall of our trailer held a scar from such a flair. It remained still when I moved out after my first year of college.

It was a typical weekend at our home, a Saturday afternoon in the summer. I remember looking out the screen door as I sat at the table, waiting for my father to sit down. I watched the steam rising from the corn on the cob in front of me. My parents had been okay as far as I could tell up to that point. Friday nights were usually spent going to the Supermarket in the neighboring town where they had an Acme, my mom's preference. My father always took my mother because she didn't have her own car to drive and because he had to pay since he never gave her any money. The entire time they were married, my mother never had any idea how much money my father made or had in the bank. Since my father was usually busy taking my mom to the store, he didn't drink as much on Fridays.

Saturday morning had seemed relatively normal. Around eleven A.M., I noticed that my father's eyes had started blinking, so I made myself scarce the rest of the day. I knew I had to show up for dinner, so I started circling our yard at a distance to see if my father was home. Unfortunately, his car was there, so I entered the house when I was sure it was close to supper time.

As a child living in an alcoholic family, you develop coping skills that provide early warning signals of danger. You must be able to walk into a room and, within a split second, read the mood of the environment and the danger level. Estimating the degree of intoxication was critical in determining when to disappear, literally or figuratively.

One of the earliest signs that my father had started drinking was his eyes. If sober, he was like anyone else, but if he was blinking every couple of seconds, it meant that he had a few drinks. If the set of his eyes was hardened, you knew that he was pretty far along. If his eyes were more open and somewhat unfocused, it meant true danger because his mood could change in a heartbeat. Upon seeing you, he was more likely to demand that you wait on him. This would start the escalation with my mother, and he knew it.

The physical stance and position of the people in the room were other clues you learned to read immediately. Tension could often be cut with a knife in our home, and to walk into the house and sense it, caused your stomach to tighten and spin circles as you looked for possible exit strategies. As in combat training, you immediately, upon entering, assess the risk and at least two possible paths to escape for your own survival. Before you let go of the door handle coming in, you need to see if you should immediately retreat.

My mother's posture and the set of her jaw showed me the tension in the air. "Don't be running off. It's almost time to eat," was her signal for me not to bolt back out the door.

My brother sat slouched in the recliner, and my sister came out of our bedroom, giving me a subtle eye roll, so I knew things were not exactly hunky dory. Glancing past her, I saw that the bathroom door was closed and heard the water heater closet door, so I knew my father was taking another drink. I had no clue how far gone he was since I hadn't seen him. As she passed me, that bathroom door banged open, and my father stood there scanning my mom for a few seconds. Tilting his head forward just a bit, as if the weight of it sent him into forward motion, he started toward me. I quickly slipped behind the table, not bothering to wash my hands as a defensive move to avoid him. His pausing, head tilt, and the redness in his face told me all I needed. He was about halfway gone on the drunkenness scale. This was a volatile area where it could go either way. It was eggshell time. Things may go okay if we all tiptoe around him and not set him off. He came in and sat at his place at the table.

Before entering the trailer, I could smell that my mom had made fried chicken, which she had placed on the table as my father took his place. Next, she placed a big bowl of mashed potatoes, a salad, and green beans. As usual, there was always some kind of bread at my father's insistence. He began placing things on his plate as we children waited so that he could get the piece he wanted. Reaching over, he took a slice of bread and looked around. My mom had taken her usual spot in the recliner my brother abandoned when he came to the table.

We children, who had started helping ourselves to the dishes available, suddenly paused, trying to figure out what he was searching to find. The tension in the room rose dramatically.

"Where's the goddamned butter?" he demanded.

I heard the foot of the recliner slam down as my mother got up and walked back into the kitchen. She had been using the butter to finish mixing the mashed potatoes and had left it on the counter. Grabbing the butter dish, she slid it across the table toward my father, then moved back to the recliner, saying simply, "There!" in an exasperated tone. My father watched as it stopped, gently bumping the side of his plate. Spinning a quarter turn in his chair, he looked back at my mother behind him. His back was to me as he faced the front door. I could see the side of his face as he glared at my mother, then turned to give the butter dish a disgusted look.

Expecting him to make some smart comment, I was shocked when he picked up his plate and hurled the whole thing at my mother, who sat looking at a magazine. The plate sailed within inches of her head, tilted vertically. It penetrated the trailer wall behind her about three feet off the floor. The walls of the entire trailer were made of a wood veneer paneling that was the color of golden oak. The plate was embedded about one-third of the way, with mashed potatoes dripping down the wall. A few green beans were stuck to the potatoes, and a chicken breast rested on the floor with a grease stain above it.

My mother looked up from her magazine, eyed the wall, shook her head, and returned to reading her article. Had she been looking up when he threw it, it probably would have scared her or caused her to hit the floor. But with her cool reaction, my father did not get what he wanted, so he stood up, walked out the door to his car, and left. The plate, complete with chicken and potatoes, was still in the same place when he arrived home drunk at eleven-thirty that night. My mother did clean it up the next day, however, having made her point and realizing he never would. The scar in the wood paneling remained a constant reminder of how quickly violence could strike.

Chapter 24
Couch Spring

My father's weekday routine was to arrive home from work around five. He would go into the bathroom, and we would hear him make himself a drink. Once accomplished, he would return to the living room and lie on the couch until dinner. It was back to the sofa when dinner was over, and he would use us like television remotes until it was time for bed. The next morning he would get up, go to work, and repeat. We tried to avoid bothering him or even talking to him. Heaven forbid if we had to ask him for money for a school trip or something else the school required.

He would have several more drinks on Friday evening but tended not to start trouble. Perhaps because he was tired from work and it was my parents' grocery shopping night. Once Saturday morning rolled around, all bets were off. He began drinking in the morning and often continued until late Sunday night.

We children had learned not to bother him during the week and to be quiet so that he could hear the television. We could work on homework or quietly watch tv, but he controlled the channel. My sister would sometimes go into our bedroom to read, but whatever it was had to be done quietly in the small trailer.

The living room in the trailer was probably ten feet by ten, and the kitchen was approximately eight feet long. My father was only about fifteen feet from the TV, even though it was in the next room. The entire couch was taken up by my father. He would lie there with his head on a cushion watching the TV positioned in a cubby space over the refrigerator. The good thing about this arrangement was that if you sat at the table, you could also watch it. No one even attempted to sit on the couch because he took the whole thing, and no one wanted to sit near him. The recliner my mom usually used was in the corner of the living room and another chair was arranged to face the couch for conversation, which meant it did not face the TV. No one ever sat in the second chair unless they were using the telephone on the end table beside it.

On this particular evening, everyone was in their usual locations. My sister was in the bedroom reading, my brother was at the table watching TV, my mom was in the recliner, and I was in my cubby hole, squatting on the heater vent. Not long after supper, my father was settled in on the couch, watching whatever his favorite show was in that time slot. He shifted on the sofa to readjust his position and get comfortable for the evening when we all heard a loud sproing. Everyone turned their head to see what made the noise. Underneath my father on the inexpensive couch, one of the springs had snapped, causing the jagged broken end to pierce through the padding and the cover. It hit my father strategically in the right cheek of his buttocks.

The fastest way to escape the sudden sharp pain was to raise his butt off the couch in a bridging position. My mom, brother, and I had all turned because of the noise, just in time to see my father bridge up off the couch yelling, "Goddamn, goddamn, goddamn!"

The threat of the protruding spring prevented him from lowering his butt back to the couch. However, the awkward position he was in, as a result, prevented him from being able to get off the couch. Once we all realized what had happened and that it wasn't particularly serious, the three of us all burst out laughing, making my father angry. He yelled at my mother, "Damn it, Shorty, do something to help me."

Infertile Ground

Seeing my father in this vulnerable and funny position was more than my brother and I could stand. I dropped down behind the arm of the recliner where he couldn't see me and covered my mouth with both hands as I writhed in fits of silent laughter. My brother ran to the bedroom laughing and must have told my sister what happened because she soon poked her head around the corner for a peek.

After examining the offending spring, my mother managed to gain control of herself long enough to snatch the pillow from under his head. She placed it under his bottom, so he could lower himself and turn to get off the couch. She then retrieved a blanket they spread over the spring as a cover. By then, I had regained some control and turned my face back to the TV, trying to act absorbed in the show.

For the remainder of the week and long after, my brother and I would lie bridging on the couch yelling, "Ooh, ooh, ooh," when my father wasn't home, to set our siblings into fits of laughter. If neither parent was around, we would repeat his expletive. We had a new couch within a week. It would have taken months to replace if it had been something for anyone else.

Chapter 25

Trips to WV

Vacations should be a time for the family to be together and go on fun adventures or to relax in some tranquil setting. At least that's what all the brochures say. I've seen or heard of cases where the kids get bored and start fighting, and the parents get tired and cranky, making vacations less than idyllic. Vacations in our family were things to be dreaded and endured every summer.

Even though we lived in Delaware and New Jersey since I was three, my father always planned to move back to West Virginia. If he had found equivalent work in the area, he would have done so immediately. So, every year, our annual vacation was spent going back "home," as my parents called it. My father always tried to schedule it around the last week of June and the first week of July so that the July fourth holiday gave him extra time. We would all be packed and piled into the car to drive the five hundred miles from southern New Jersey to the general Charleston area of West Virginia. My mother's and father's parents lived about thirty-five miles from each other on opposite sides of Charleston.

The trips occurred in the mid to late 1960s, before the interstate highways in that area were completed. This meant we had to travel on interstates around the Wilmington, Baltimore, and DC areas, then hit secondary roads once we got near the mountains of our destination. These were winding, mountainous roads from when we left Virginia until we arrived. It was a grueling twelve-hour trip on a good day. We would usually get started early in the morning, which meant my father started out drinking coffee. We kids would be slumped in the back seat, usually trying to sleep. However, memories of past trips and the excitement of seeing my grandparents and cousins made that problematic for me. That, plus the fact that I was the youngest, meant that I had the middle of the back seat. If I fell asleep, I would be abruptly awakened by an elbow as soon as I leaned in one or the other direction enough to touch either sibling. There could be no whining because that would set my father off. If you had to pee, you held it unless it was a dire emergency. If you did have to go, it would be by the side of the road where everyone could see you.

 My father drove ninety percent of the time, regardless of his level of intoxication. Even when he drove, the drinking began as soon as the clock slid past noon. Any troubles or delays that lengthened the trip would increase both the travel time and the level of intoxication upon arrival. As mentioned, this was the 1960's and my father was one of those macho types who "knew how to hold their liquor" and "could drive better drunk than most people could sober." So, on trips to West Virginia, his level of intoxication was highest on those treacherous mountain roads. When we got closer to "home," he occasionally pointed out spots where he or another of his friends had crashed a car at a particularly tricky turn.

 Adding to this general terror, usually by his second or third drink, he and my mother would begin arguing. It could start over anything, such as him yelling at us kids to be quiet or my mother trying to make a point that he should not continue to drink.

 If a man at a gas station happened to look too long in my mother's direction, she would be called a whore for taunting the guy. It was scary enough when they argued at home because at least there was some physical separation between them. Still, in the car, everyone was within reach of my father's swing, and blows were not uncommon during these trips. My father usually drove recent model Lincolns that he would buy used. My mother, a small woman, could sometimes get against the passenger door and be far enough away from him that he had to work to reach her. I remember a few times when she swung her feet up on the seat and used her legs to push him against the driver's door.

Perhaps this would be an excellent place to slow down and remember that three children were in the back seat. My oldest sister had moved out long ago. We were on dark, treacherous mountain roads with a drunk man at the wheel. I can picture my father, red-faced and screaming at my mother. Calling her a whore for flirting with the man at the gas station who was more likely looking at the car of New Jersey northerners as he walked to his beat-up pickup. My mother would be yelling back at him, asking what the hell she would want with another man and what about all the whoring around that he had done during their marriage. I remember staring through the windshield at the rock face beside the road, whizzing past. I watched it coming closer when my father swerved off the road edge or over the white line (the center lines were not yellow yet). Cars would go by in the other direction with their horns blaring. My sister, and occasionally all three of us, would be screaming, .

If this was not terrifying enough, when my mother decided she had enough, she would tell him to stop the damned car. He would invariably ignore her. After demanding a few times, she would open her door and threaten to jump out of the moving car as he sped along the mountain road. I remember leaning forward and trying to grab her arm to save her. Behind her, I saw the road's edge speeding past through the opened door, my mother's foot perched on the doorframe inches from the asphalt. At this point, all of us would be screaming at him or her to please stop fighting. I can remember wanting to be transported anywhere, sure that I would watch my mother jump to her death or we would all crash and die.

A few times, my father did stop, and my mother would get out and start walking away from the car. I sat there thinking, "Don't leave us with him! Are you nuts? What about us?"

If she walked ahead of the car, he would follow her, trying to talk to her or calling her names. If she went behind us, he would get out of the car and stagger back to confront her, leaving us in the car, inches from the traffic lane with cars and trucks whizzing past us. Usually, the cries of the kids snapped her out of it or perhaps the realization she had nowhere to go. If she returned to the car, she sat sullen and angry, trying to ignore him as long as possible. If he let her drive, he would sit brooding as she lit into him for several miles. Usually, if he was drunk enough to give up control, he would pass out before too long. We would sit like silent little mice until we got to where we were going, likely only to sniffle occasionally as we tried to regain control.

We would usually go to his parents first. My mother would spend an obligatory few days visiting. His parents lived in the tiny unincorporated town of Seth along the Coal River southeast of Charleston. She loved his parents but ultimately wanted to escape him, so he would take us to her parents in the small town of Dunbar just west of downtown Charleston. My sister usually stayed at my Grandma Patton's and was closer to that side of the family. I always went with my mom because her dad was one of my favorite people, and I had cousins who lived near them. My brother did a little of both and showed no preference. My parents barely communicated during these visits, and my father would only stay for a night at my mom's parents. He never got out of line because he respected my grandfather and grandmother Droddy. He occasionally misbehaved at his parents' home, so I felt much safer at the Droddys'.

As the time to return drew near, the tension grew. There was always resentment after the battles during the vacation. Still, my father knew he had to work and usually waited until the last minute to go home, so he was less likely to drink hard. They were more likely to ignore each other as much as possible or be terse with one another. That's not to say there weren't a few knock-down drag-out fights on the trip home. You never knew what to expect. Since the last part of the trip home was on interstates and heavily patrolled, my father had to be more careful.

Chapter 26

Driveway Fight

During our vacation when I was around seven years old, we survived the trip to Seth. Having been there a few days, it was time for us to go to Dunbar. My father had been on an absolute tear the day before to the point that he had made my grandpa Patton angry. I have a picture of my grandparents sitting on a little bench in their yard taken when we were loading the car. My grandmother is smiling forcibly at the camera. My grandfather sits staring straight ahead, obviously not thrilled at having his picture taken.

Since I was delegated to the middle of the back seat, I had to get in first. I had just gotten in the car and could hear my parents arguing as they loaded luggage and bags into the trunk of the Lincoln. The trunk lid was up as I turned to look because it sounded like they were at a fevered pitch. My mother demanded to leave a day earlier than initially planned because of my father's behavior toward his father the day before. My grandfather scolded my father about his behavior the previous day, and my father threatened to "knock him on his ass." My father was about five foot seven inches and weighed around two hundred pounds. In comparison, my grandfather was five foot, two, and perhaps one hundred and fifty pounds. I had never seen my father show such disrespect, and the whole family was shocked and angry.

He began complaining about her wanting to leave early, and she ripped into him about his drinking, his disrespect, and the example he had set for his children. I could only see their waists through the crack under the open trunk lid and then my father's back as he retreated so my mom could put something on the driver's side of the trunk. I am not sure what exactly triggered it. Perhaps he was angry about being corrected by her or felt guilty about being such a jerk to his father. She had started around the driver's side of the car, demanding the keys saying he was too drunk to drive. Suddenly, out of the side of the back window, I saw his right arm cock back, and he swung at my mother. She slammed back into the car's fender and sank to her knees.

I started yelling, "Mom! Mom!" as I scrambled to get over my sister because her door on the passenger side was still open. She was getting out because she had heard the thump of my mom against the fender, suspecting something bad had happened. She was moving too slowly for me because I knew what had happened and wanted to get there as fast as possible. I didn't know what to do, but I would try something.

I rounded the car ahead of my sister and saw my mother sitting on the driveway, leaning against the car. Her eyes were unfocused, and her face was covered in blood from a cut above her eye. My father usually wore a square-shaped ruby ring with a small diamond in the middle of it on his right hand, and it had cut her eyebrow. She reached tentatively with her left hand to touch the wound. My father stood above her, fist still clinched, glaring at her. I saw my brother behind him, the car's rear door open, as he yelled at my father. My sister behind me was screaming at the top of her lungs.

I was sure Mom was mortally wounded. There was so much blood. The fear inside me was overwhelming, and I had no idea what to do. I remember saying to her, "Mom, please don't...." I couldn't even say the word die. Then I realized I shouldn't say such a word to a hurt person, so I completed the sentence by saying, "be hurt." What a dumb thing to say. She was obviously hurt. What was I thinking? I prayed she hadn't heard me. I prayed she wouldn't die.

I felt my sister push past me and try to help her. I glanced up to see my nine-year-old brother run up and punch my father in the back to no effect, so he put both arms out and tried to push him away from my mom. My father must have snapped out of his rage between the screaming and the pushing because he took a tentative step back, looking around. I followed his gaze and saw his parents coming through the gate at the driveway's end, his father yelling, "What the hell is going on out here?"

My father spun and headed for the house to get another drink. When my grandparents came around the car and saw my mother, I heard my grandmother cry, "Oh my Lord!" Then she rushed to my mom's side. They both knelt to help my mother, who was just regaining her senses, and tried to stand up. My grandfather and sister caught her arms and steadied her against the car. Her blouse was covered in blood, and my grandmother ran into the house to get a towel. Meanwhile, my sister grabbed a hand towel or something from the trunk and gave it to my mother.

My grandfather moved me out of the way, so he could take my mother into the house, as my brother and I both cried from fear and anger. As they approached the bench in the yard, my mother realized where they were headed and said, "Oh no. I'm not going in that house with that son of a...." She must have realized who she was talking to because she stopped and finished it, "with him!" They sat her on the bench, and my grandmother came out with a wet washcloth and a towel. She tried to clean up my mother, but it was evident that she needed stitches.

I was so traumatized by the incident that I can't remember how she got to the doctor or how we were transported to her parent's house. I remember she had a black eye for the rest of the vacation. I was sure this was it. They would get a divorce, and then where would we go? Would we stay at our grandparents, or go back to New Jersey? I wasn't sure which frightened me more, going back to live with my father or facing the unknown. When it was time to return to New Jersey, my father showed up very repentant. I was shooed out off the back porch and into the house as I heard my grandfather say, "Now, Red..." as my father hung his head.

My feelings were muddled. I wondered how my mom could even consider returning after what he had done. Still, I was also relieved that I would return to my familiar school and friends. I heard her talking to her parents when I was in another room, saying the words that always drove a stake in my heart, "if it weren't for the kids." I hated that I was the one that was condemning her to live with that monster. I promised myself that I would never hit my wife if I ever found someone who loved me. I would never hit any woman. How could you call yourself a man if you hit people weaker than you?

On the trip home, he didn't drink, even when he got an earful from my mom the first few miles. The air in the car was tense between them, only exchanging what needed to be said. All of us were mad at him and gave him terse answers when asked a question. I hoped this might change things for him and he would stop drinking for good. I imagined him being so sorry that he would change his ways, but by the next weekend, he was drinking, and soon he was back to his old ways.

Chapter 27
"Oh, Shorty, look what they did!"

I always hated my father's hands. They were a constant threat to me and others I loved. His left hand contained a mangled ring finger from his mishandling of a pistol. He had used his hand to steady the weapon shooting at a bottle while standing in a rowboat. Instead, he managed to shoot through his finger. Drunk again, of course.

One of those weekend nights when I lay in bed, unable to sleep because he was still out drinking, I heard his car pull into the driveway. I immediately went to my defensive posture, covers up to my chin, back against the wall of pillows, and my head under my own. I peered through the little crack I kept beneath it. Oh God, I wonder how drunk he is and what will happen tonight.

I heard the car door slam, but it seemed to take him a while to enter the house. I didn't hear any singing meant to wake the whole neighborhood. What could this mean? Inside it was complete silence. We were collectively holding our breath. After several minutes the door slammed against the porch railing, and I could hear my father's heavy footfalls but at a faster-than-normal pace. He didn't announce himself as usual but headed straight back through our bedroom, and as he passed, I caught a glimpse of him holding his left hand by the wrist with his right. He held it out in front of him, and there were streams of blood down both hands and his wrist as he plodded toward the bathroom. I heard him go to the sink and turn on the water.

"Hey, Shorty, help me!" he shouted. My mom ignored him, probably assuming it was another attempt for attention.

"Shorty, goddamn it, I cut my finger off." I heard my mother stir and enter the bathroom.

"Oh God," I heard her say, "How'd you do that?"

"In the damned car door, but I couldn't find it in the dark."

By now, we were all awake. My sister and I stood beside the bed, afraid to look, and my brother peeked over the bunk bed rail. I heard my mom say, "It's not gonna stop bleeding. Wrap your hand in this and keep it over your head. We need to get you to the hospital." I heard the splashing of her running a washcloth under the water.

Mom poked her head around the corner of the bathroom door and said, "Annette, take a flashlight and go see if you can find your father's finger in the car door."

"Really?"

"Yes, damn it. He's made a real mess."

My sister reluctantly dressed in a robe, grabbed a flashlight, and went outside. My father must have been in pain because I heard him groan and say, "Hand me my medicine." He was talking about his bourbon. By now, I had stepped into the bathroom and saw him with a bloody wet washcloth wrapped around his hand.

"Don't you think you've had enough?"

"Goddamn it, this fucking thing hurts! Now, hand me my medicine!"

My mom went to the closet containing the water heater and handed him a half-pint he had there. He opened it and took a swig from the bottle. He usually mixed it with some water.

I turned to see my sister enter the trailer carrying a bloody paper towel. "It fell out when I opened the door." She extended her arm toward my mother, looking like she might vomit.

"Wet the towel, and put it in a plastic bag with some ice," my mom instructed. A look of disgust came over my sister's face, and she turned back to the kitchen. I heard her opening the refrigerator and wrestling with the ice trays. My mom began herding my father out of the trailer as she did that. He stumbled back through the trailer, arm in the air, carrying the half pint in his other hand. My mom argued with him, saying she couldn't drive with an open container in the car, but to no avail. She took my father's index fingertip from my sister, and they went out the door. He had severed it at the first joint.

My parents didn't return until three in the morning. We slept restlessly, and both went straight to bed when they came in. The next day they slept in late, so my brother and I managed to disappear before my father was awake. My father took it easy on the drinking the next day, and he had a bandage on his finger that wrapped around part of his hand. It wasn't until Monday that we got the entire story of their trip to the hospital.

They had managed to save the tip of the finger and sew it back on. My father wiped out the half-pint going to the hospital and was a handful for the staff. He was belligerent, with the nurses alternating between flirting and cursing them out. When the doctor came in, my father was not exactly thrilled that he was Asian, and he told the doctor he was a World War II vet that had fought against them (even though he had served in Europe). My mother heard all this from the waiting room as she tried to make herself invisible in the chair.

Finally, an exasperated nurse emerged to retrieve her because my father was making a scene. When she returned to where he was being treated, he sat with his arm laying on a stainless-steel tray. A towel covered his upper arm with his wrist and hand exposed. My mom came around the corner and, in a whispered scolding, asked him, "What the hell is wrong with you? These people are trying to help you."

He turned his head to her and, with tears running down his cheeks, cried," Oh, Shorty, look. Look what they did. They done cut my arm off."

They had given him a mild sedative to calm him down and had numbed his arm at the shoulder so that he couldn't move it. Mom simply lifted the towel to show him it was still attached. As my mom told the story, she had tears in her eyes, describing the look on the nurse's face as they both tried not to laugh. It was a story she would use against my father with visitors if he started bragging or acting macho to bring him down a notch or two.

Chapter 28
Swimming Lesson

Once we were old enough, all of us kids would scatter, and we rarely did anything as a family. However, in these early years, there were times when we still were forced to do things together. One of the activities that required parental supervision is swimming. I recall several times when we went to a swimming hole, as my parents called it. The first place I remember was a canal that eventually ran out to the Delaware river in Deepwater. It was near the entrance to the turnpike. Several events happened there that I remember.

When I was real young, and my brother had first learned to doggy-paddle, he used to tease me by swimming close to me and splashing me. This was a constant irritation, and I had no real recourse to get him back. My mother used to love to tell the story of when he kept doing this as I became angrier. I finally reached my limit when he did it again, and I did the only thing I could. I pulled down my swimming trunks and did my best to pee on him, screaming, "Goddamn, goddamn, goddamn." This was to the apparent amusement of all the adults in the area.

The second thing I remember from that swimming hole was my brother looking out and seeing a turtle's head poking out of the water in the middle of the canal. It was about thirty yards out in the water. Always up to a challenge, he decided to swim to see if he could catch it. I heard him yell, "Look, a turtle," as he took off swimming. Knowing I couldn't swim, I was envious of his ability to go after it. He swam out about ten feet when suddenly he turned around and started frantically returning to shore, his eyes the size of saucers. After he had gotten on the shore, he turned back to look. When I asked him what happened, he simply said, "Snake!" and pointed to a water moccasin whose body we could now see gliding on the surface. We watched as it turned away from all the people on the shore and went in a different direction.

Once we moved to Handy's Trailer Park, we went several times to a swimming spot on Game Creek Road. It was near a kid's farm that I knew from school and had a reputation as a place where people drowned. It was man-made from people removing sand to sell and was very deep in places. We tended to stick to the shallow edges as my parents watched us splash around to get cool on hot days. The farms in the area employed many Puerto Rican farm workers who had also found that spot to swim, much to my father's disapproval. I remember the last time we swam there, one of them went missing. We sat on the shore watching the rescue crew dragging the lake for the body, eventually finding it in the deep part.

I was fascinated by the process, but as soon as they brought the body up, my mother covered my eyes, and we left. This was fine with me because seeing it at a distance left me with no interest in watching them pull it into the boat or to shore.

The last place we ever went swimming as a family was near a rest stop on the New Jersey Turnpike. It was only a couple miles from where we lived, and there was never anyone there. The rectangular body of water must have been dug as part of the groundwork for the rest stop. No stream fed or drained it, so groundwater must have fed it. My brother found it while exploring the area on his bike with Sug. My mom was sitting on a blanket, and my brother was swimming around. My sister stood at the edge up to her knees and wasn't thrilled with the experience.

Of course, my brother started taunting me and splashing me with water. I moved closer to my father, seeking protection, and asked him to tell my brother to stop. My father simply said, "What's wrong? It's only water."

"He doesn't like to get his face wet. The little baby," my brother mocking me, said. It was true. I didn't mind sticking my head underwater, but as soon as I came up, I would wipe my face with both hands, trying to clear my vision and breathing as quickly as possible.

To my complete surprise, upon hearing this, my father reached out and grabbed me around the waist. He picked me up, saying, "No son of mine is going to be a little sissy."

He then proceeded to try and shove me under the water. Deathly afraid, I struggled to keep my head up. My father placed his hand on my head, pushed me under the water, and held me there. I had no idea how long I was kept under, but it had seemed like an eternity. I had struggled so desperately that no air was left in my lungs.

Finally, he released me. I broke away from my father as fast as I could. I was furious and frightened, but my father and brother were laughing. Determined never to let that happen again, I went out the next day with his friend Hawky and taught myself to swim. We went to a small pond beside the road just below the Jennings family's house. It was not very big and had a small sandy beach on one side. It was part of a creek that ran through the area, so the road had culvert pipes about four feet in diameter on the street side. Since it was deeper there, I started from the sand and imitated my brother's doggy paddle. Soon I could swim from one side to the other. Once comfortable, I began sticking my face under the water and raising it back out without wiping it. I soon realized that if I tossed my head as if trying to move my hair out of my eyes, it cleared the water. By the end of the afternoon, I was swimming underwater with my eyes open and having fun. No one could ever hold me under again, I swore as Hawky and I lay on the warm blacktop in the sun. Only one house stood at the far end of the Quillytown Road. It had originally continued, but was cut in half when the New Jersey Turnpike was built. Since it was a dead-end now we weren't worried about traffic.

Chapter 29
Welding Side Jobs

My father's welding skills earned him a good reputation in the community. He would often take on side jobs on the weekends to do welding and pull mobile homes for people. The benefit for us was that he made some extra money, tended to drink less, and could only start drinking after finishing the jobs. Any delay in starting was good because it usually reduced the amount he would drink.

My brother helped him occasionally when he was younger. Thus, my brother knew much more about welding and mechanical things than I did. But, as he entered his teen years, Buddy was less likely to volunteer or agree to be recruited for my father's outings. I, however, decided at an early age that going with my father on errands or side jobs was a bad idea.

One of my first experiences was a trip to get a Sunday paper. I was excited because we took the truck, in which I rarely had a chance to ride. It was when we still lived in Delaware, so I assumed we were going to a local convenience store, but instead, he went to a liquor store. He told me to stay in the truck, and I watched as he disappeared into the store. The liquor store was attached to a bar. I wasn't sure if he went to the bar or was chatting with the sales clerk, but he was gone quite a while. I remember sliding off the bench seat and, at five years old, resting my chin on the metal dashboard of the mid-fifties Chevy. I began to get concerned as I watched car after car pull in and then leave on each side of the truck. I smiled at the first few people when they waved at me. But after what seemed like hours, which was probably thirty minutes, I was convinced I had been abandoned. I wondered what would happen to me because I had no money to call my mom, and I wasn't sure I remembered our number. I sat staring at the phone booth in front of the truck, wondering if I should ask someone to call my mom. My only other option was to look for my father, but he told me kids weren't allowed in liquor stores, so I was waiting in the truck.

I managed to work myself into such a state that I was crying when the next car pulled in beside us. The other driver went in and came out with a look of concern on his face. I tried to wipe away the tears so they wouldn't know but based on the look on his face, I guess it was obvious. Finally, I saw my father standing near the front counter, paying for a newspaper. It suddenly occurred to me that I had better not let my father catch me crying. He would likely call me a little sissy, so I frantically dried my eyes. I found a rag under the seat, where I knew my father kept some and wiped my nose. Scrambling back onto the seat, I tried to look casual as he came out the store door and passed the front of the truck. I could see his eyes blinking as he approached the truck. They hadn't been before, so he had a drink while inside.

My father opened the door and threw the paper on the seat between us, then tossed a few packs of gum of various kinds down too. He looked at me as he pressed the starter button on the cab floor and said, "I knew it wasn't my boy that the man said was crying outside." Then he winked at me. "Want some gum?" he said, nodding at the seat. I couldn't believe I had gotten away with it. We drove home, and as I slid out of the truck and closed the door, I stepped up on the running board to look in the oversized side mirrors at my face.

All around my eyes was a deep red, with smudged tear marks down my cheeks. Then it occurred to me that I saw no other children in the cars outside the store. I couldn't believe he had let me get away with my attempted deception. Instead of going in the house for several minutes, I acted like I was busy, then ran over to the hose and washed my face. After checking in the mirror again to ensure my eyes were back to normal, I went inside. I can probably count the number of times I went with my father again to get the paper.

The few times I was drafted to help my father with something cemented my determination to make myself scarce before being roped into it. Whenever he did anything, he seemed to take the longest time possible to accomplish the least amount, especially at home, because he would stop at every step for a drink. He had the two saddlebags on his truck that he made from plywood that were about six by two feet, and I swear he would drag every tool out of each of the boxes just to tighten a bolt on the handle of a lawn mower. It was a totally exasperating experience to work with him. No matter how small the job, it would occupy your entire afternoon if you got roped into helping him.

God forbid, you had to go anywhere to do something with him. In addition to his habit of dragging out every tool, you would never know where you would end up or how many stops you would make before you would returned home. As a ten-year-old, I can recall sitting in the seat of that same truck as he said, "I need to make a stop up here at whatever." I would feel like my head would explode because three hours into this misadventure which he promised would take fifteen minutes, we still had not arrived at the supposed job site. Thus, every weekend morning, it was a race to see if my brother and I would escape before we could be roped into anything. We got our chores, such as lawn cutting, done during the week.

It was always a bruising experience when I could not escape because I would inevitably do something wrong or not understand what he asked me to do. If he asked for a specific tool, there was a fifty-fifty chance that I was unfamiliar with it. This might have explained his preference for my brother's help because he knew more than I from helping more than I did. I would usually come away angry or with my feelings hurt, or both when he told me I was stupid and would never amount to anything.

My father would probably have been considered a master welder, which could explain his impatience with a ten-year-old who didn't know one end of a torch from another. He had worked for years in the shipyards honing his skills. I personally saw him work on everything from heavy equipment to bicycles. I have heard stories told by my uncle of my father welding a shaft down inside of a transmission backward by using a mirror.

Chapter 30

No Mechanic

I frequently watched my father, brother, and Sug work on motors. Engines fascinated me, but I was also intimidated to try to do any repairs. Even though I had been riding the little 50 cc Honda for a few years, I had never done much besides put gas or oil in it. I could check the tire pressure, add air, or change a taillight bulb or turn signal. But the motor and its workings were like black magic to me.

Even though I knew the basic components, carburetors, pistons, valves, etc., how it all came together seemed like something you shouldn't mess with. Because the little Honda was so reliable, there was never really any need for me to attempt anything. However, being a curious young boy and having come to learn to love the motorcycle as much as I did, I wanted to learn how to maintain it. My curiosity finally got the best of me one day, and I decided to check the spark plug on the little bike. I don't remember if it was sluggish starting or anything was wrong. Still, I opened the small tool kit, took out the spark plug wrench, and imitated what I had seen Sug do a few days earlier with his 305-cc Honda. What could it hurt?

When I took it out, I wasn't sure what to check, but I simply cleaned off what little burnt carbon deposits were on the tip, and I knew it was supposed to have a certain gap but had no idea what it should be. Since it had been running, I assumed it must still be close. Feeling proud of myself and more competent, I reinstalled the plug. I noticed that going back in, it didn't feel as smooth turning as it had coming out, and it seemed difficult to tighten. When I tried to start it, it wouldn't fire. Oh crap!

When my brother came home that day, I reluctantly told him the bike wouldn't start. Being an older brother, his first question was, "What'd you do to it?"

Thinking I shouldn't lie, I reluctantly told him the truth.

"Oh, jeez. Great job, moron, you cross-threaded it. It's probably ruined."

Oh no. This meant my father would learn about it. I was sure I was a dead man. We had not spent a dime on the little Honda since we had bought it, other than gas and occasionally oil. I knew he would never pay money to fix it since I was the only one that rode it now that my brother had the Zundapp.

Sure enough, when my brother told him that evening, he had a fit. "How could you be so stupid? Why would you mess with something that was running just fine? If you don't know what the hell you're doing, don't touch anything!"

I was humiliated and brokenhearted at the loss of my little motorcycle. I wondered how I would learn anything when no one showed me, and all my father ever did was yell at me. He repeated my brother's words that I had ruined it for good and to never touch anything around there again. He referred to me playing with a Dennis the Menace hand puppet I got for Christmas one year. He said, "You better stick with playing with your dolls because you'll never be a mechanic."

Two days later, he brought home a set of metric taps he borrowed from someone at work. He reset the threads for the spark plug, and the little Honda fired the first kick. I was so glad that I hadn't ruined the little motor although I had to endure another lecture about not messing with things if I didn't know what I was doing.

Having reinforced my fear of messing with motors, I always brought any issues to my brother or Sug. I would never ask my father again. After the obligatory abuse from my brother about being useless, he would reluctantly help me with whatever issue I had. While I showed decent mechanical skills at other things, including the rest of the motorcycle components, I always treated the engine as a black box not to be explored. As an adult with today's high-tech engines, I still do it reluctantly, preferring to work around the periphery rather than dive into the engine's guts.

Chapter 31
Mickey's New Talent

From the time I was young, we always had a dog. Usually, we only had one because, like most people of that time, my father believed dogs should live outside. When I was in elementary school, our dog was an Eskimo Spitz named Mickey. He was a medium-sized dog with long reddish-brown hair and white on his face and paws. We kept him tied outside with a doghouse like snoopy in the cartoons. He would always greet us when we came home from school, and we would occasionally let him off the leash to run around and play with us. Mickey was a fast, fuzzy, obedient dog with eager eyes and a bushy tail. My father liked him because he had reddish hair, and I'm sure that was why my parents picked him up from the pound.

However, my father didn't pay much attention to the dog unless he drank. Then he might go out to visit it and stand talking as Mickey looked at him attentively, likely listening for the few human words he had picked up like "treat" or "dinner." He was the perfect company for my father, who felt ignored and misunderstood. Mickey didn't usually get to go for rides in the car since we only took dogs to the vet when they were sick. Mickey usually rode in the back with us kids when he did and enjoyed the constant attention.

One particular Saturday, we played with Mickey in the front yard, and my father came out. He was going to the store to get some cigarettes and asked if anyone wanted to go with him. We all quickly declined and acted like we were preparing to leave on our bicycles for somewhere important. I was walking around the front of the trailer holding Mickey by the collar to go tie him up. Mickey's ears perked up when my father opened his car door, and he pulled toward the open door. I jokingly said, "I think Mickey wants to go."

To my surprise, my father turned around and slapped his leg. "C'mon, Mickey," he said enthusiastically to the dog, likely glad someone wanted to go. I let go of the collar, and the dog shot into the car and perched himself in the middle of the front seat. I laughed and watched as my father pulled out of the driveway, Mickey smiling back at me because he got to go for a ride.

I didn't see my father again until I returned for supper that evening. Mickey was back, chained in his usual spot. My father was standing on the sidewalk near his car as I tried to quietly slip into the trailer before he noticed. He turned to face me as I hit the bottom step, "Mike, come here." His face was flushed, and his eyes were blinking, but his posture was mostly normal.

"How was Mickey's adventure?" I asked, trying to disarm him from whatever command he was about to make.

"That's the damnedest dog," he said. "He got into my peanuts and ate every one of them." He didn't say it like he was angry. It was almost as if he was impressed. My father habitually kept some kind of snack for himself in the car, usually under the front seat. It was typically a bag of pork rinds, or "pork skins," as he called them, or a bag of unshelled peanuts.

"Did he eat them shells and all?"

"No. That's the thing. He shelled them and even took the paper off 'em," he added, pointing at the back seat. "I'm gonna need you to clean this up after supper."

I looked in the car, and sure enough, there were peanuts shells and dark brown paper pieces all over the back seat, the floor, and the passenger side of the Lincoln. I couldn't help but laugh in amazement.

After supper, it took an hour to get all those little pieces of paper cleaned up. We never noticed if eating all those peanuts had any harmful effect on the dog. Mickey seemed unaffected by the misadventure and continued to like peanuts after that.

Chapter 32

You Weren't Wanted

I grew up feeling like my mother was the only thing between me and utter chaos and despair. I knew she loved me, did everything she could to get us what she could, and protected us from the monster that was our father. She was the rock in the storm of my father's alcoholism, and I was frantically devoted to her. My father understood this because we children, and especially me, were always on her side. My sister often tried to distract or placate him, which made her seem less biased. My brother would try to stay out of it as much as possible unless my father got physical, then he would join us in protecting my mom. I would avoid my father as much as possible and always be on my mom's side, giving him looks of disapproval when I could do nothing else.

My father would try to find ways to undermine this devotion, often trying to tear my mom down in front of us. When he was on one of his rants about her alleged infidelities, he would talk about how she would wear what he called short shorts and parade around flirting.

I had never seen my mom look at another man, let alone flirt. The only thing I had ever heard her mention was the actor Clint Walker and how she'd just like him to pick her up so she could fall asleep in his arms like a little baby, and I was shocked when she said that.

My father often said that he was sure I wasn't his child, and then my mother would say that I looked just like him. When she said it, it hurt me more than it stopped him. His answer was that she slept with his brother Owen. It was a repeated insult thrown at me. I was too ugly to be his kid. He would scream it at me if I tried to defend her or argue with him about anything. All this did was further alienate me. I shouldn't have had to deal with his grief if I weren't his kid. I would tell myself that it improved the odds that I wouldn't grow up to be like him, which was my greatest fear.

The cruelest thing he would say to me was that my mother never wanted me to be born. The interaction usually started with him and my mother arguing. As it degraded into name-calling and accusations, he would ultimately call her a whore. She would counter with all the times he cheated on her and even throw in a few names of women she had either caught him with or that she had been told about. As things became more heated, his body language became increasingly threatening. One of the children, likely me, would start voicing concern asking my mom not to fight with him or for him to leave her alone.

Several times when I was between the ages of ten and twelve, he tangentially redirected his anger at me by yelling, "Why are you defending her? She didn't want you."

I remember him pointing that mangled finger of his left hand at my mother. "She tried to get rid of you." Then he looked at me to see my reaction.

Seeing the confusion on my face, my mother pleaded, "Now, Red."

He looked at her and immediately realized he had found a soft spot. "When she was pregnant with you, she would sit in the tub soaking for hours, trying to cause an abortion."

I had no idea if this were true or if it even would cause such a thing to happen at my young age. When I looked at my mother, she had tears flowing down her cheeks, and her expression changed from shock at the betrayal to anger.

My father drove the dagger deeper, "That's how much your mother wanted you. She tried to kill you before you were born."

The rage getting the best of her, my mother shouted, "Can you blame me, you son-of-a-bitch! Can you blame me for not wanting to bring another child into the world to grow up with you as his father!" Then she started crying and stomped out of the room.

I felt absolutely hollow. I stood, trying to absorb the information I had just been assaulted with. Was it true? Did my mother not even want me? Her reaction to his words showed that it was likely. Could I blame her for not wanting a fourth child? I couldn't logically, but it didn't dull the blow. The bell could not be unrung. The seed I would carry for life that I had been unwanted had been planted.

I never hated my father more as I looked at him in disgust. Even at my age, I realized what a horrible thing to do to your child.

He stood there with a satisfied smirk on his face as I turned and walked out the front door, so numb that I couldn't feel my feet on the sidewalk. I walked through the trailer park, into the woods where my friend Hawky and I had built our tree fort and climbed into it. I lay down and sobbed until I couldn't cry anymore.

I would not let that bastard see me cry. I would not let him know how deeply it cut. I cried until I fell asleep, and when I woke up, it was dark. I felt a sense of panic at being out after the street lights had come on. I would be in big trouble. Then remembering, it didn't matter. Instead of running home, I took my time. When I saw the driveway, my father's car was gone. Entering the house, I could see my brother waiting for me to be yelled at by my mom, sitting in her usual chair in the living room.

"Are you hungry?" was all she asked. My brother was dumbfounded.

The next few times he tried it, my mother was more prepared for the assault and could deflect it and continue her arguments. He eventually gave it a rest but had done his damage and went on to other tactics.

Like most things in my family, my mother and I never discussed it. Issues like that were buried along with the other hurt that grew like a mountain, every weekend, every weekday of knife-edged silence, year by year, half-pint by half-pint of bourbon.

Chapter 33
Close Encounter on the Delaware

One of the last times I remember my brother going with my father was when my father announced he was going fishing. I have no idea what possessed my father to do this. Perhaps he had caught the opening of an Andy Griffith show rerun on TV or felt guilty about never doing anything with his boys. Maybe he just wanted to go fishing. My brother agreed to go. At the time, he was about twelve. I refused and was called a little sissy by both of them.

Since they didn't have fishing licenses, he decided to fish in tidal waters. In New Jersey, you didn't need a fishing license in tidal waters (this changed in 2008). They scraped up some half-baked fishing gear we had lying around, and off they went. After searching for a good spot along the river where you were both allowed and had access without walking a long distance, the brilliant idea was proposed that they rent a boat. They found a place to rent one somewhere on the Delaware side.

The boat was a small, open boat, perhaps twelve feet long, with a small motor and oars to reposition the boat once you found a spot. My brother had never been in a boat on such a large river. My father had a boat similar to the one they rented back in West Virginia. Still, his experience was on the Coal River behind our house in Seth, which was nowhere near the size of the Delaware River. The Delaware River also has commercial lanes for ships headed for Philadelphia and Trenton.

Our two-brave sailor/fishermen went boldly forth, putting out into the river. They tried to find a primo fishing spot in the general area above Pea Patch Island, where Fort Delaware is located. Some boats go back and forth to the fort for tours. Private boats are not permitted to use their docks. They found a spot my father liked, so they shut off the engine. My brother threw out his line while my father whipped out a pint of bourbon and settled back for some quality father-son time.

The day was warm but not too muggy, and there was just a hint of a breeze on the water. My father relaxed as the water lapped against the boat's side, enjoying a new perspective of the world on the river. They agreed they should do this more often. My brother only got a few bites because his equipment was meant for a lake or pond fishing and not for the river environment. Still, he felt entertained by the few nibbles he got . Meanwhile, my father enjoyed another drink or two.

In the late afternoon, my brother noticed that the ferries going to the island seemed to have stopped. Our brave fishermen hadn't really managed to get started until almost two o'clock. As time passed, Buddy drank the soda, ate a sandwich they brought, and wished he had something else to drink. They hadn't noticed that the little boat had drifted below the island and into the shipping lanes. When the shadows of the trees on the shoreline started getting a little longer, they decided they had better head back. My father told my brother to fire up the little motor and take the helm.

Having received only brief instructions onshore, mainly directed at my father, my brother attempted to start the little two-stroke engine. He could barely get a sputter out of it. He started to get nervous as my father started barking out instructions, not amused at his inability to bring the engine to life. His arms burning from pulling the rope, my brother tried again and again with the same result, and the instructions turned to insults at his inability.

Railing at my brother's incompetence, my father gave it a few cursory pulls. Frustrated, he declared that my brother had flooded the damned thing in his ineptitude. They will just have to row back. My twelve-year-old brother grabbed the oars and started trying to row back to the shore. The current of the lowering tide had them in its grip, pulling them out toward the bay at a quick pace. My brother could make no headway against it and couldn't even keep the bow headed toward the shore because of the engine's drag, which acted as a rudder. He began to panic as the realization hit him. Meanwhile, my father was finishing off the bourbon to brace himself against the chill of the failing light and the breeze picking up.

They switched places in the boat, my father's drunken fumbling making even that maneuver frightening. Upon moving, my brother noticed a large ship approaching them. They are now dead center of the shipping channel and being pulled straight toward the freighter. As my father tried frantically to row, my brother stared back at the ship looming in the dusk. It grew larger and larger until he looked up and could see the cresting wave of water curling off its bow.

Realizing he was getting nowhere against the tide, my father stood and pulled the cord on the engine again. My brother glanced back at the ship bearing down on them, sure they would be killed. My father lost his balance and steadied himself by placing his left hand on the top of the engine. The movement caught my brother's attention because it came close to his head, like the threat of a blow. He followed my father's hand down to the engine, then noticed a tab on the side of the engine with an arrow pointing to "off."

"What's that?" he asked my father, pointing to it. My father didn't hear him because of his own exertion and panic. Curious, my brother reached over and turned the indicator in the opposite direction. It didn't move easily but did rotate. The next pull by my father made the engine sputter. On the second try, it caught and started.

Unknown to my brother, my father had turned off the gas as instructed. Unknown to my father, my brother turned it back on. My father grabbed the throttle and threw himself in the rear seat, causing the bow to rise. Throwing the tiller as far to the right as possible, my father opened the throttle wide. My brother crawled on the boat's floor toward the front to balance. The small boat shot toward the shore. My brother, lying in the bow, watched the ship as it filled the horizon to the east.

When they finally reached the rental place, it was dark, and the manager scolded them and said he almost called the coast guard. Surprisingly all my father said was they had trouble restarting the motor. He acted almost sober, and my brother noticed his hands were still shaking. Once in the car, my father pulled out another half-pint and took a drink directly from the bottle instead of mixing it with water as usual.

Even though he had been sworn to secrecy, my brother told me all the next day. My father spilled the beans the following weekend when he was drunk again. My brother never went with him after that. My father never again offered to take us fishing.

Part Three

Teen Years

The teen years are a struggle for any kid. Your body is changing, hormones are raging, and you are trying to find your place in the complex social scene that becomes more important to you. Angst and insecurities are at their peak as you begin to learn to interact with the opposite sex, driven by internal urges you've yet to understand. Being thrown in with a chaotic and abusive home life magnifies the struggle by numerous factors.

Fear and embarrassment prevented me from having friends from school visit knowing that my father would be drunk and humiliate me. At this point, I considered it a positive that we lived so far from town that I could disappear into relative isolation. My friend Hawky witnessed some of my father's behavior first-hand and accepted me. He quickly learned to limit his exposure and wasn't there in the evenings when things were at their worst. I only had one or two friends in high school that ever came to my house, and it was usually to pick me up from the driveway or drop me off, and even that was rare.

I knew early on that I would never be able to bring a girl home without suffering humiliation, either by my father being a jerk or making inappropriate comments or advances toward her. Dating for me was out of the question. It didn't help that our home life had seriously hampered the development of some ordinary social skills that likely had eliminated me from consideration by most of the female population. I often joked that wolves raised me, so I am often unaware of many subtle social mores.

As my brother and I grew older, we were viewed by our father as a bit more of a threat, at least based on his behavior. Even though I was only about one hundred and twenty pounds soaking wet during my high school years, I shot up to five foot nine inches by the time I was about fourteen, making me an inch or two taller than both my father and brother, but I was a stick. My brother was about five-six but still chubby and always stronger than me.

Chapter 34

Old Man Betrayal

Only once did my mom side with my father against my brother and me. As we both hit our teen years and spent more time around the Jennings boys, we picked up some of their habits and phrases. Everyone was referred to as "slick," as in, "Hey, Slick, hand me that wrench." Someone we considered not right in the head was called "flicted," as in afflicted. One of the other terms they used to refer to their father was "old man." They would use it when speaking to him, not behind his back. Sug might say, "Hey, old man, where did you say you wanted that tractor moved to?"

It wasn't long until my brother started using the term on my father. Initially, it didn't seem to faze my father at all. He would even respond to it, usually with a begrudging comment when he was sober such as "I'll show you old." Since my brother got away with it, I also joined in referring to him that way. It was easy for us to bring him down a notch and not use the term, Dad. I never called him that, as I didn't think he deserved it.

We continued to call my father Old Man for probably half a year, using it more often until he put the brakes on one day. It was early Saturday afternoon, and my father had only a drink or two, usually just enough to mellow him a little. My brother and I had just come in from playing a game of touch football and were both riled up from fighting with each other since we were never on the same team. I don't remember what my father said to us, but my brother turned and said something like, "Take it easy, old man. I need to use the bathroom first."

That set my father off. "Boy, get your ass back in here. I'm talking to you. And, Mike, you'd better goddamn listen too. I don't want you calling me 'old man' or slick or anything else but dad or father anymore. Do you understand me?" He stood up from the couch, glaring at us, fists clenched. I saw him glance over at my mother, who sat looking from him to the two of us.

"Answer me, goddamn it! You hear me?"

"Yeah," we both mumbled under our breath.

"Don't mumble at me like a couple of little pussies. If I hear one old man out of either of you, I'll slap the piss out of both of you. You understand?" He felt like he had us on the run and always had to push it—another glance at my mom, who sat silent but shot a quick look at him.

We started to both turn away.

"Answer me! Now!"

It dawned on me as I watched the interchange between my father and mother that she had put him up to it, thinking it was disrespectful of us to use that name. Of course, he would go overboard to prove what a tough guy he was, especially since he had her permission to go after us without her jumping in to defend us. I was shocked and angry at my mother at that moment. I saw the look on her face turn to fear as my father took a step toward my brother and me, which brought me back out of my head.

"We heard you," I said almost simultaneously with my brother.

"You heard me, what?"

"We heard you, sir," I spit the last word out like a bitter pill, refusing to use any other title. I would have taken a fist to the mouth before calling him dad or father to his face.

"That's better." His smug look made my skin crawl, and I shot an angry look at my mother, who had betrayed us. I looked in the refrigerator as if I wanted something, then shot out the front door as soon as it was clear. My brother was headed out the back door, and as we walked together into the edge of the woods, he said, "She put him up to it, you know."

"I know." After my anger subsided, I thought about it and gradually concluded that she was right. Knowing it was disrespectful, I was shocked that the Jennings boys got away with it. I realized that if my mom had sided with him, it had probably gone too far. She was trying to teach us respect that would help us in life. Like everything else, we never talked about it. Our family corrected us by swats on the nose rather than logic.

Chapter 35

Ghost Horses

After our dog Mickey died, my father, mom, and brother came home one Saturday from the pound with a dog we named Sam. Sam was a larger dog, probably eighty pounds, a mix of collie mostly and a little German Shepard. He had the gregarious collie personality and looks. I was surprised that his bark was higher pitched than I expected, which made him sound less frightening than his size might suggest. He would bark, and his whole body would wiggle when we came home from school, making it hard to resist going out to give him a pet.

Sam was also a good watchdog who would bark at anything unusual in the area. He didn't bark incessantly, so the times when he did, you knew to look around. There were a few incidents at night when Sam would bark, and after a while, you might hear a car door close or the rattle of garbage cans from raccoons trying to find food. If he barked too long, I would hear my mother yell at him to be quiet so the neighbors wouldn't complain.

One night, I heard him barking frantically but was too lazy to get up and look outside. My mom yelled at him a few times, and he would be quiet for a few minutes, then start up again. Finally, I heard my mom get up and stomp through the trailer on the way out to quiet him down.

The following morning when I got up, my mom sat bleary-eyed at the table drinking coffee.

I made myself some tea and sat at my usual spot. "You look tired, mom."

"That damned dog kept me up half the night. Didn't you hear him?"

By then, my sister and brother were rummaging around in the kitchen. "Yeah," I answered, "I heard him bark some."

"Well, he was barking like a crazy dog, and I went out there with a broom to beat his ass." Sam was such a big dog that my mom employed a broom to be more threatening. She wasn't an imposing figure at five foot two, but she was hell with a broom in her hand. Sam had countered this by digging out all the dirt under his doghouse. It had the benefit of catching water in the summer rains, where he would lay in to get cool. It also provided a place to hide when my mom threatened him with a broom. I'm unsure why he felt safer under the doghouse than in it. If he was barking, all my mom had to do was come around the corner of the trailer, and if she had a broom he dove for cover.

"You're mean to that poor dog," my sister said as she searched the refrigerator.

"The rest of the night, I had nightmares about them damned horses," my mom said, staring into her coffee cup.

"What horses?" the three of us said almost in unison.

"The horses that ran through our yard last night." She looked at us incredulously. "Didn't y'all hear 'em? They scared the shit out of me."

"Horses? In our yard," my brother looked at her skeptically. "Yeah, right."

"Yes. I'm telling you, there were horses, and they almost ran over me. I had to run around the back of the shed to get away from them."

"Was this in your dream?" My sister sat down, interested now.

Infertile Ground

"No! It wasn't in a dream. Sam was barking, and I went out there to quiet him down. It was foggy so that you couldn't see Miss Cole's trailer (Our elderly neighbor across the street). I was standing there, ready to beat his ass, and suddenly, these three horses came out of the fog into the yard, running right at me. Sam ran under his doghouse, and I ran around the back of the shed where they wouldn't fit."

"Did you get into Dad's medicine?" my brother asked again.

"No! I've never touched that stuff, and you know it."

"And you weren't dreaming or sleepwalking?"

"No! I swear to God."

"You're messing with us." He looked around the table at my sister and me. "How come none of us heard any of this?"

"How would I know? I don't know how you could sleep through it. They were out there, whinnying and running around. Go look at the tracks if you don't believe me."

"So, you're telling me there are horse prints in our backyard. Right now."

"Yes."

"From horses that came out of the fog and chased you into the house."

Annoyed now, she added, "I said yes."

"Bull hockey," my sister said.

My brother laughed. "You're just trying to trick us into going out and looking."

"I'm telling you what I saw. I don't really give a damn if you believe me or not or if you go and check or not." I knew she wouldn't push a joke this far.

I was sitting by a window facing the doghouse, so I turned around to look. The ground looked disturbed around the area the dog couldn't reach, but I wasn't sure there was evidence of horses. "There's something out there that might be hoof prints."

"Yeah, right. You're probably in on it." My brother remained unconvinced

"I'm gonna go look," I announced, standing up and squeezing past my mom.

"Yeah, yeah. Have fun."

I walked outside and started around the front of the trailer. Glancing out at the dirt street, I saw three sets of hoof prints approaching our trailer. It was obvious where they went around my father's car even though it was gone now. I followed them to the back of the trailer. Then they went straight to where the dog was tied. You could see where they stopped and milled around a bit, then took off through the trees toward the back of the trailer park, where the woods started.

While returning to report my findings, I saw my friend Hawky riding his bike across the yard. "Hey, Hawk. Have I got an adventure for you. Come on." I went inside, waving him in. "There's horse tracks out there, alright. They go off into the woods."

"They were probably chasing the elephant I saw last night." My brother rolled his eyes.

"What?" Poor Hawky was confused.

"Well, we're gonna track 'em," I announced. I quickly heated up a couple of cinnamon Pop-Tarts in the toaster, asking Hawky if he wanted any, wrapped them in a paper towel, and headed back outside. "Come look at this." I filled Hawky in as we examined the prints and petted Sam.

Grabbing our bikes, we first checked the direction the horses had entered the park from the road. They had briefly spent some time in Miss Cole's yard, then made a beeline for our backyard. We tried to track where each horse had gone, but the tracks intermingled so much that it was hard to keep them separate.

We followed them down the dirt street of the park to where it ended and became a rough two-track the owner had made with his bulldozer. We left our bikes at the end of the path where the undergrowth started and tracked them on foot for another fifty yards where the prints just stopped.

"They had to have gone back," Hawky said.

Infertile Ground

"But the tracks only went in one direction. It doesn't make sense." We walked in an arching pattern from the last clear tracks to see if we could pick up the trail again. After twenty minutes of trying ever-widening arcs, we gave up.

"Whataya think?" he asked.

"It's like they disappeared." I shrugged. "There's only one answer," he looked at me. "Ghost horses."

"Yeah," he agreed with an exaggerated head nod.

We went back to our trailer and reported to my mom and siblings.

"You two have ghost brains," my brother said.

"The tracks are out there. Go follow 'em yourself."

When my brother finished eating and dressing, he walked outside. You could see the surprise on his face at the sight of the tracks.

"They came in from the road up at the entrance," I volunteered. Buddy ignored me. We watched him follow the tracks down the dirt street to the dozer path. Then he disappeared into the woods. He didn't return until supper and never said anything about what he found. I knew that if he had been able to follow them, I would have never heard the end of it. He said nothing about it other than to tease my mom whenever the subject came up. He would ask her what animals had chased her the night before. I would join in now and then. We never did solve the mystery.

My mother would laugh and only say, "You saw the tracks."

Chapter 36
Annette's Realization

Even though she tortured me as a kid by setting off my hair-trigger temper, my sister, Annette, was kind and optimistic. It showed even more later in life. She was always the peacemaker in the family, jumping in to try to distract my father when he started trouble. She always hoped to have that fairy tale father-daughter relationship that you used to see on TV. It was never to come.

When she was about sixteen, my father had to take a trip to West Virginia in the winter. I think it was when his mother was battling cancer and was having an operation, but I don't remember that detail. My mother decided to stay home so my brother and I would not miss school. It was going to be a quick trip over an extended weekend and my father's cousin, Garland, who had lived in the area for a while, decided to go with him. My father and his cousin's relationship was usually okay, but both could become belligerent when drinking and had fought each other before at a family get-together.

My sister had always been close to my father's mother, and I assume for that reason, she decided to go with them. She thought she would sleep in the back seat, and in no time, they would be in WV, an easy trip. What should have been a twelve-hour drive took close to twenty hours. A snowstorm that swept in from the west caused the delay. Tired, my father and Garland also decided to stop at a bar halfway through the West Virginia leg.

My sister took a pillow and a quilt to make a bed in the big backseat of the Lincoln my father currently drove. After over an hour, the car began to get cold as she waited in the winter storm outside the bar. The temperature dropped and snow began to cover the trunk and windows. At sixteen, she knew she wasn't allowed in the bar, but they had been in there for a long time, so she decided to see if they would let her check on them

Throwing back the quilt and opening the door, a blast of arctic air greeted her. She walked gingerly to the bar's entrance. There were a few windows, small and placed high in the wall. Condensation obscured the windows and beer signs. She couldn't see inside to look for him, so she went to the door. Gathering her nerve, she opened it and stood just inside. The smell of cigarette smoke, stale beer, and body odor hit her as she tried to adjust to the dim light.

Several patrons at the bar turned to leer at her. Even wrapped in a heavy coat, she felt them undressing her. Pulling her collar tight around her neck, she managed to spot my father, and Garland seated just a few tables away. They were with two hard-looking women. The table had a collection of beer bottles and a few glasses in front of my father. Garland had his arm around one woman's shoulders, his head back, as the woman ran her right hand on his chest under his jacket. My father sat leaning toward the other woman whose hand was on his left leg.

"Daddy?" she barely heard her voice over the din of the jukebox and conversations. "Daddy, I'm cold out there. Are you coming soon?" she added more forcefully. The woman talking to our father looked up and said something to him, lifting her hand from his leg and pointing at my sister.

He didn't react at first other than to stare at the hand pointing and then back at the woman's face as if he wasn't sure what she had said. His eyes squinted a bit as he tilted his head in drunken confusion. My sister took another step toward them, not daring to look at the bartender or the frightening patrons there. Seeing a cup on the table, she thought he might get her something warm to drink.

"I said, is that your daughter?" the woman raised her hand, so it was level with my father's eyes. He followed her hand as it ascended, eyes blinking staccato in their telltale sign.

Finally turning his head toward where she pointed, he glanced casually toward my sister, then back at the woman. "She called you daddy."

He thrust his bottom lip up as he shook his head. "Never seen her before." The woman's forehead wrinkled, and she glanced up in time to see the devastated look on my sister's face.

Annette stood there as the realization of what her father had just said hit like a fist, her mouth still open, and tears streamed down her face. She covered her embarrassment with her hands as she spun in place. She heard Garland's voice, "Annette, darling, sit down. Let me buy you a Coke." Her head spun as she tried to focus on the door, her escape route. A chair scraped across the wood floor of the bar. As she opened the door, she half turned to see if it was Garland trying to catch her. The bleach-blonde with her father stood, palms out as if to push him away. Our father was protesting the woman leaving, not even a second thought for his daughter.

The white world outside was blinding, and Annette stood with her hand on the doorframe for a few seconds, recovering her balance. She wanted to run away somewhere or to be home in her bed. Surely this was a nightmare. She saw a phone booth at the corner of the building, but who would she call? She was at least four hundred miles from home. Her grandmother was sick, so there was no one she could call to come to get her. Not even sure of the name of the small town they were in, what would she tell them anyway?

Then the crushing pain of the betrayal brought another wave of dizziness. Her own father had denied knowing her. Just so he could do what? Sleep with that skanky bleach-blonde? Oh my God, the level of depravity. Who was this man? How could he do this to her, who she thought was his favorite?

A gust of frigid air knifed through her coat and accented the tear tracks on her face. Man, it was cold. She stumbled back to the car, focusing only on the back door. Fumbling with the door and falling into the back seat, she wrapped the quilt around her and fell face down into the pillow, allowing herself to relinquish control, and bawled into the pillow. Her sobs came from a place deep inside her, almost primal in their grief. The death of her innocence was the price she paid. She cried herself to exhaustion and sleep.

When she awoke, Garland was driving. He was the soberer of the two. Her father soon passed out in the passenger's seat, head against the window. My sister glared at the monster she could reach and touch as hurt and rage rose within her. For the remainder of the trip, she refused to speak to him unless necessary and then in clipped phrases as short as possible. She dared not burden her grandmother or tell anyone so that it could get back to Grandma until she was better.

Annette held it until she returned home. We could immediately see that something was wrong since she did not greet us with her usual enthusiasm. I purposely stayed near my mom until they separated from my father and Garland when the story came pouring out of my sister. I wanted to scream for her and hurt my father. I wanted to hug her and tell her we all loved her and would never deny she was a part of us. But we never did such things in our family, so I just listened, tears in my eyes, trying to absorb the pain from her, wondering how we would all ever heal.

Chapter 37
Inventing Specialized Lathe

My father never missed work, no matter how much he drank the weekend before or how late into Sunday night he rampaged. He would get up Monday morning, puke his guts out, and go to work. I can never fault him as a provider. He could be a self-centered, stingy bastard, but we didn't go without food or shelter.

From what I could tell, his co-workers highly respected him. It made sense because he was a pretty good guy to other people when he was sober. There was always some residual tension from the weekends that his goodness didn't necessarily extend to family members. The Delaware Memorial Bridge, which links southern New Jersey with Delaware, ran beside the DuPont plant where he worked. As we rose above the complex when driving past, he occasionally pointed out some significant structures he helped build as a pipefitter. As kids, we thought it was cool and always tried to look for them as we passed.

My father would score some major points with the company he would be able to bank on later in his career when I was in my early teens. The company used some sort of pipes made of a special composite material in their chemical processes. I assume they had unique characteristics to deal with the specific chemicals running through them. From what my father told us, whenever they wanted to connect these pipes, it was a complicated manual process of preparing the pipes for the joining process. They had to cut each end of each pipe by hand. Each end took the workers about forty-five minutes, and the cuts were not always correctly done.

My father had the idea to make a lathe specifically for this process, and with his boss' permission, constructed a prototype of one from scraps they had lying around the yard. His welding skills and construction background helped him create a lathe that cut the time to less than five minutes per end and produced more consistent quality, saving the company millions. The company patented the machine and made millions more on it. Since he created it at work, with company materials, my father did not even get his name on the patent but did win significant points.

Dupont sent him to drafting school and offered to send him back to college to get an engineering degree. However, my father turned them down. I do not know why he declined, but I highly suspect it resulted from his PTSD. After being promoted to sergeant in the war, my mother told me later that he tended to avoid situations where he was responsible for others. Completing a degree would result in a promotion to management. After dealing with losing men in battle, he did not want to (or could not) deal with that kind of responsibility again.

Chapter 38
Wrestling

When my brother was a senior in high school, he decided to go out for wrestling, so I also signed up. He wasn't exactly thrilled with my decision, but I think it made it easier for my mother to talk my father into letting us. We never participated in any after-school activities because we could not get home afterward. It meant that my mom had to agree to pick us up using my father's car. It also complicated our dinner schedule. My mom had to start dinner, then leave to pick us up at four-thirty. My father usually got home around that time. We would be back by around five when we usually ate. So, dinner had to be pushed back a half hour, which made it a big deal to my father. Somehow, my mom talked him into it.

Since my brother outweighed me by around forty pounds, we never had to be paired up in practice and managed to avoid each other as much as possible. I weighed approximately one hundred and eight pounds and enjoyed the workouts and the drills. I was not a great athlete by any standard, but I learned quickly, so I did well during practice because I found it fun.

Our first match came during a Christmas tournament when I

wrestled a kid from another school. It was only an exhibition match because neither of us had made varsity, and the coach was still deciding on the JV squad. My troubles started when I went to weigh in since I was wrestling the one hundred-and-six-pound class. The regular conditioning during practice had added some muscle to my scrawny frame, and not being used to dieting, I came in almost a pound heavy. I could see the coach wasn't happy. We only had forty-five minutes until the match started when we could be re-weighed, so I did calisthenics in the shower, wearing a rubber suit the whole time. I made weight barely but was dehydrated and exhausted as a result.

When it came time for the match, it was as if I was in a different world. My vision felt blurred around the edges, and the noise from the crowd roared in my ears. Several matches were going on simultaneously in the gym, so the crowd's noise had nothing to do with what was happening in my bout. My hands shook, and I felt a bit faint, both from the dehydration and the adrenaline. In my head, I could only hear my father's voice telling me how weak I was and how I would never be any good at anything. I tried to convert it into anger to direct it at my opponent. My arms felt sluggish and slow, my hands tingling as if numb. I struggled not to throw up. Despite all this, I lost only three to five against my opponent.

I was relegated to the practice squad but did wrestle a few JV matches that season, winning one. In mid-season, they had a Parent's Day. I have a picture of my parents with me in my wrestling uniform. It was the only appearance my father ever made at our matches. I look like a scarecrow . My mom is the only one smiling, and my father wears a drunk smirk and was caught in mid-blink in what has to be one of the most awkward-looking family pictures ever taken. My brother's picture was a little better than mine.

His attendance resulted in my father mocking both of us regarding our practice during warm-ups of shaking our arms with our hands hanging slack to keep our arms from being tight and stiff. Whenever he would bring up wrestling, suggesting it was a silly waste of time, he would stand and shake his arms with a drunken smirk. So much for parental support.

I lifted weights and ran during the summer, putting on about ten pounds. As a result of the varsity one-hundred-twenty-three class member of our team who had been state champ the year before being disqualified for drug use, there was an open spot. I was one-hundred-eighteen soaking wet, but the coach had me compete for the position. Since I always did well during practice, I managed to win the spot. I was varsity. When it came to my opponents, most of them looked like gorillas compared to me, having worked their weight down from one-thirty or more to wrestle what was a very competitive class.

I spent my junior year battling as best I could but ultimately over-thinking, having my father's voice in my head, and wrestling over my weight, ending in a poor result. My coach signed my yearbook saying, "you'll win one next year."

Determined, I worked out again all summer and learned much from a former teammate who returned from college and showed us some cool moves. I was ready. Christmas tournament, I used some of my new moves to battle fiercely in the first round. I lost five to seven against an opponent who ended up sweeping the whole tournament, with mine being the closest match. I was still nervous going in but had managed to tune out most of the noise in my head. Because I had lost, others could challenge me for my position by the coach's rule. The JV kid challenged me and hyper-extended my right elbow during our match. I finished and won using one arm, but the coach could see I was injured and replaced me. My arm never healed enough during the season, and I had trouble with it for years afterward. It would lock, slightly out of place, and I would have to stop and rotate it around in the socket to pop it back. It took a lot of physical therapy and strengthening of the muscles around it to eliminate the problem, and it still aches when the weather changes.

Chapter 39
Siblings Leave

.

After Annette graduated, she left for the summer to visit Ritzie who was now in North Carolina. She managed to get around needing my father's permission because she turned eighteen a month before graduation. My sister also didn't mention how long the visit would be. When she returned, my father hit her with his speech of my house/my rules, trying to exert at least some control over her, although my sister never gave them a bit of trouble that required him to do so. She found a job that helped her to spend less time at home and gave her more independence. Annette got married the September after she graduated high school, but unlike my oldest sister, she chose her husband carefully. Fred was a good guy, college-educated, and treated my sister well. My father was not enthusiastic about the marriage because Fred was also a head taller than him, which I think he found somewhat intimidating. They moved to an apartment in town, completing my sister's escape from my father's influence.

My sister was wildly happy, and you could see her blossom outside the pressure cooker of our home life. Since she lived right down the street from a friend, I was a frequent visitor at their apartment and became closer to Fred. They both had jobs and were well on their way to building a life. Watching them interact and enjoy their home life gave me hope that there might be something like that waiting for me in the future.

Back at home, the dynamics had been interrupted because we no longer had Annette's influence over my father, trying to distract and joke around with him. My brother, now seventeen, worked with my oldest sister to procure a car and now had more freedom. He and my father bumped heads about curfew, but it never escalated too far. My brother had always tried to be invisible when the trouble started, and the few times we had only brief conversations about my parents fighting, he blamed my mom as much as my father. Our views were very different and having lived in a strained environment for so long, we didn't get along that well. We had always been rivals and fought a lot as kids.

The huge blowup between my brother and father happened the spring before he graduated. My brother announced that he would join the Marines as soon as he turned eighteen, which was in June. My father tried to get him to consider community college, but my brother said he didn't want to attend college. My father had never considered college an option for either sister, assuming they would just get married and have babies. Buddy's choice was his way of ultimately thumbing his nose at my father. He wasn't going to college and had shied away from high-school college-prep classes, opting for shop classes instead. He also wasn't joining the Army, which had been the branch in which my father served. The Jennings family influenced his choice of Marines because Mr. Jennings had been a Marine in World War II, and so had their son Michael who was killed in Viet Nam. The Jennings family always revered Michael as a hero.

My brother was my father's namesake, his heir. After my brother left for boot camp, my father railed against the Marine Corps on several successive drunken weekends. The insult had landed squarely, hurting my father. This betrayal resulted in my father taking the savings he had put away at work for college and buying himself a new (used) car and a camper (tent trailer). Upon his announcement of this decision, I sat there thinking, "uh, what about me?"

I had been the one taking college prep classes all through high school and doing well. Our highest honor students were all girls, but I would be one of the higher-ranked boys. I was the one who promised himself that he would make it to college and have a better life than this. What was I supposed to do? After realizing where he stood, I knew it would be up to me to find a way to get to college. I went to my guidance counselor the following week and told him my situation. He said he would do his best to help me find a way, and what I had to do was to keep my grades up and work hard.

Chapter 40
Stepping Between

With my brother gone, the dynamic shifted again, with just my mother and I left to be the targets of his abuse and demands for attention. No one else was left to protect my mom, and with my physical growth, I had no choice but to step in between them. I was all of five foot, nine and one hundred and eighteen pounds, a stick. My father was probably around two hundred pounds in his middle age and stood at five-seven.

Our confrontations occurred when he attempted to get physical with my mom. After watching as a helpless child while he gave her black eyes or choked her up against a wall, I had promised to stop him when I could. I was fifteen when my brother left. Shortly after that, during one of their usual weekend arguments, my father caught her between the table and the white metal cabinet where we stored the dishes. He had pushed her against the cabinet, making her stumble. Then he grabbed her right arm with his left, and his right hand reached for her throat when I grabbed his shoulder and pulled him backward, sliding my hand down his arm. Turned sideways now, he turned to look at me, surprised.

"No," I said. "This isn't happening anymore. Leave her alone."

Anger replaced the surprise on his face as he spun to face me. "Oh. So, you're a big man now. Tough guy wrestler, huh?" I took a half-step back, keeping my eye on his hands, expecting him to throw a punch. He opened and closed his fists several times, deciding what to do.

"I don't want to fight you. But you're not going to hurt her anymore."

"You worthless piece of shit. There's no way that you're my son." I could hear my mom yelling at him to leave me alone. "You think you're a big man, but you'll never amount to anything. You hear me?"

"Come on, Mom." I risked a glance at his hatred-filled face. If he was venting and throwing insults, he was less likely to take a swing. I had my hands up in front of me with open palms to indicate I was no threat but also to block any blows. My mom slipped past him, so we were both facing him. "Let's take a walk, Mom."

She turned and went out the door, and I side-stepped so that I would not turn my back to him. It was late afternoon, the sun at an angle across the yard. My father followed us out as far as the steps. He stood yelling, full of bravado. "You'll never be anything but a loser your whole life. No woman's ever gonna want you, you worthless little bastard. If you ever lay a hand on me again, I'll put you in the ground."

We walked around and visited with an older woman who lived across the street, my mother re-living the whole story as she listened attentively. She was a devoutly religious woman and vowed to pray for us. He was asleep in the back bedroom when we risked going back home. It was a Sunday, so he went to work the next day. We never mentioned it again, though he was exceptionally curt with me for the next week. I gave him a wide berth to reinforce that I was no real threat.

His physical attacks were reduced after that, at least when I was around. He may have been waiting for a chance to get her alone. The other major confrontation we had, I was outside but could hear them arguing. I kept my attention on the pitch of the battle inside to make sure it did not get out of hand, but I had learned long ago that I could not affect their arguments. He sounded pretty far along, which had me concerned. A sudden change in intensity and a thud from inside caused me to shoot up the steps and inside.

This time they were on the other side of the table, in front of the refrigerator. My father had his left hand around her neck, and his right arm was cocked and ready to punch. They were slightly sideways to me, so I rushed forward, putting both hands on his right shoulder, and pushing him into the refrigerator. He lost his balance and went down to his knees, letting go of her, and she moved behind me. I stepped back, my arms up, trying not to be threatening now that the danger had passed. He turned to face me and returned to his feet, using the refrigerator and a dining room chair to balance himself.

"You fucking, no-good little bastard. You think you can take me?" He was faster than I expected, for as drunk as he was. He was throwing a punch with his right hand. I blocked it with my left, and since my hands were inside his, I grabbed the front of his shirt with both hands and lifted it until he was off-balance, throwing him back into the refrigerator again with the same effect. He was on his knees again, and I backed up, holding my hands in the same defensive position, trying not to threaten him.

Up quicker this time, his face was crimson with the veins standing on his forehead and neck. "You miserable son-of-a-bitch, I'm gonna teach you a lesson you'll never forget." This time he rushed toward me, trying to grab me, but since my arms were inside his, I caught him again and threw him down. He was on his ass this time and sat there for a few seconds collecting his bearings; it had happened so fast. Cussing me again, he got up to his knees.

By this point, I was so frustrated and angry at what he had said and done that I stepped toward him and drew my right fist back. His face was level with my waist, and I was in the perfect position to lay him out for good with just one punch, and I intended to end the insults and the threats by doing it. He would be helpless. I growled, "Stay down, old man."

I have no idea what snapped me out of it, perhaps it was the thought that he was in a vulnerable position, but I realized that I was about to punch my father in the face. That went against every value that my mom had taught me. It would also take me down to his level and make me just like him. I dropped my hands, turned, and walked out, my mom following behind me, asking if I was as okay. As we walked, I told her how close I had come to hitting him.

"I'm glad you didn't. You'd never forgive yourself. I'm proud of you, son."

Chapter 41

Swimming Upstream

Later that same year I talked my parents into letting me stay home alone while they went to West Virginia for vacation. As the youngest of the family, it was the first time I would stay by myself for a week. What could possibly go wrong?

I stood in the driveway and watched as my mom's worried face disappeared around the first corner of their journey. The sun was breaking through a blanket of cloud covering after three days of heavy rain. I took it as a sign. Freedom! I could do anything I wanted. A flood of options went through my head, most of which I knew wasn't possible because my neighbors would report me. We lived in a small community where anonymity lived only in the dictionary.

My brother left for the Marine Corps earlier that summer, and my youngest sister was now married and living in town. I figured she would stop by to check on me during the week. I decided to ride my bicycle down to see my friend, who lived about a half-mile away. I had been cooped up in the house because a bad storm had blown through earlier and was glad to have an escape. As I started down the usual path through the low-lying woods, I found it swamped by six inches of water. Turning around, I took the long way on the road.

Water flowed in the gutters along the path and lay in puddles in low spots. It had been a toad-choker the past few days, and there was nowhere for the water to drain. Branches lay broken from the wind, scattered across yards, and along the edge of the roadway.

When I got to the Jennings house, I found that Hawky wasn't home, but Sug was outside. Sug was a year older than me and had a more athletic build. He always hung with my older brother, so this was an unexpected surprise for me.

"Hey, Mike Patton, you want to go with me?"

"Sure," I said. "Where are you going?"

He nodded his head toward the creek that ran behind their property. Their small farm was bordered on two sides by roads, one going north/south, and one going east/west. The creek ran from one street to the other in an arc, probably a quarter of a mile long.

"I want to go see how high the creek is on that road." He pronounced it as 'crick' like many others in this part of South Jersey.

In that part of the state, not much money was spent building bridges across the many creeks in the area. The road levels tend to follow the natural landscape, and the counties put large pipes to contain the flow of the usually small waterways. These pipes are typically four feet in diameter, which they surround with rock and concrete, then build the roadbed on top. In both places where the creek intercepted the street, the roads dip about fifteen to twenty feet, crosses the waterway, then raises back up to continue. Typically, the water flows lazily along and through the pipes. On the rare occasion that we have a large amount of rain, however, these low spots often flood with the water going across the street anywhere from a few inches to a few feet.

From where we were standing, we could see the water looked about three feet deep across the road, making it sketchy to ride a bicycle through, or even a low car. With so much water moving, the current was particularly strong and fast. Sug wanted to go down to where we could check out exactly how deep it was.

"Sure. Let's go," I answered, excited by the opportunity.

We started down that way, and I noticed as we walked across the pasture that he picked up a five-gallon oil container that had floated up on the rising water.

"What's that for?" I asked.

"You'll see." It was a metal container that had a lid that screwed on one side of the top and a spout on the other.

As we got closer to the flooded portion of the road, you could hear a roar emanating from someplace. The water was higher than I had ever seen it. I couldn't believe it moved that fast. When we reached the edge of the mocha-colored water, he kept walking. I stopped to assess the current, but seeing that he had no trouble standing, I continued behind him. By the time we reached the edge where the creek usually started, the water was up to our knees, and the current pulled heavily on the legs of our jeans. I became aware the roaring I heard was caused by a vortex in the water where each four-foot pipe was. The water overwhelmed the culverts, and the suction created by the flow through them, caused this vortex to form. I watched as small objects came floating down the creek, circle the vortex like a drain a few times, then get sucked down and disappear.

Sug stopped and said, "Watch this." He held the five-gallon container over his head and tossed it close to the vortex. I watched in amazement as the large container circled, then disappeared into the whirlpool. You could hear the metal can bang as it travelled through the pipe ten feet below us. You could tell exactly where it was because of the violent noise. I felt a tapping on my arm and looked to see Sug pointing at the other side.

"Three, two, one!" he said. The oil can shot up at least three feet out of the water on the other side.

"Holy crap!" I shouted. "That was cool."

We watched as the can circled lazily in the eddy floating near the edge of the creek. I ran to get it, and brought it back to Sug, struggling to walk upstream against the current. As soon as I handed it to him, he tossed it near the whirlpool again. We stood and watched it disappear then listened to it bumping through the pipe. It shot out even higher this time but was lost in the eddies on the other side of the creek.

"Can you imagine being sucked down there?" he asked.

I shuddered. "Ugh, horrible." I thought about it for a minute, then asked, "Since it's only about thirty seconds, do you think you would live through it?"

He pointed at the can in the creek. "Look at that thing. It's all scraped up and dented from hammering against the pipe. Even if you survived, you'd be knocked out and drown. They'd find your body tangled in some bushes downstream."

We stood looking at the vortex, each entertaining gruesome thoughts.

"Is this the highest you've ever seen it?" I asked, trying to banish the thoughts from my head.

"Pretty close." He pointed to a large oak tree near their chicken coop. "It once came almost up to that tree. If it had gotten any closer, we would have had to teach the chickens to swim." The water was a good ten feet below the tree. Sug's entire family was prone to enhancing the truth, always trying to reel an unsuspecting sucker into believing some tall tale. He had just tipped his hand with the chicken swimming line, and he knew it. "What do you say we go check out the other road?" he said by way of diversion.

"Sure. I'll bet it's even higher over there." We turned and started up the road. We stayed on the blacktop to avoid the muddy fields, and walked to the crossroads, then left to the other end of their property. It took us about ten minutes. We wandered down the center of the unmarked pavement because we knew there would be no traffic. It felt post-apocalyptic to be walking down the middle of a road with no concerns with on-coming traffic, not that there was ever much so far out in the country. We were five miles from the nearest town and a mile from any interstate in the farm country of southern New Jersey.

When we arrived at the other water crossing, the creek spilled wide across the meadows, running so deep that it looked almost still. As soon as we stepped into the shallow edge, however, you could feel the current swell against your ankle. The uniform of the small cluster of boys in the local area, for summer, was jeans, a green t-shirt, and no shoes. We tried to go all summer vacation without wearing shoes. We had calloused feet that could handle the heat of a blacktop road, and boasted a farmer's tan on our arms.

Sug turned to me with his eyes wide with excitement. "Let's swim to the other road."

"Are you sure it's safe? That water is moving pretty fast." I grabbed a small stick and threw it toward the middle. It was swept away quickly, spinning in the current. We both watched as it disappeared around a bend in the creek, hidden by bushes and trees.

Sug started wading in, and pointed ahead of him. "Look. We'll use that log as a life raft." He gave me no time to think before he was up to his waist, then swimming toward a ten-foot section of a tree trapped in an eddy near the edge.

"Wait up," I yelled as I splashed into the muddy stream.

We both made it to the log, and threw an arm over it. As we swam to the middle of the current, holding on to the log, it began to spin around. The water was cold and I felt my breath catch as I adjusted to the change.

"If we both get on the same side of the log, maybe it won't spin as much," Sug said over his shoulder. I hesitated, wondering who exactly was supposed to switch sides. Since he didn't move, I tried to pull myself up to straddle the log, but as soon as I would put my weight on it, it would roll. That meant I had to go under it, and I wondered if I'd be able to hold on and move to the other side at the same time. I grabbed it with both hands and ducked my head under in the brown roiling water. I could feel branches from submerged trees scraping my jeans A wave of panic went through me as I envisioned a broken twig snagging the denim and pulling me under. I came up coughing, trying to clear my face of water and leaves.

"You okay, Mike?" A quick concerned look came from Sug as he struggled to negotiate the creek and keep us pointed downstream.

"Keep your feet out in front of you, so you can push off anything we come in contact with."

"Got it." Once we gained some control of the makeshift raft, it started to be fun, and we were amazed at how fast we were moving. "We'll be at the other road in no time," I shouted. "Then let's do it again."

As we neared the apex of one turn, we could not stay completely clear of the small tree branches protruding from the water. Both of us reached to push ourselves away, sliding our right hands along the vegetation. We were focused downstream, glancing only long enough to place our hands against anything that would give us purchase, moving from branch to branch. Out of the corner of my eye, I saw Sug shaking his hand. At the same moment, I felt my skin come alive. It was as if a thousand people were each tickling my hand with a feather, the sensation rushing quickly up my arm. I looked and found my arm was covered with ants, spiders and other small insects of various species. I thrust my hand into the water and swirled it around. When I pulled it back up, most of the insects were gone. I shoved it under again and scraped it against the log, removing most of the rest.

Looking at the trees, we were passing, you could see that they were covered with every insect imaginable. Spiders, ants, grasshoppers, anything that lived in or on the ground had sought higher ground. Good grief. I quickly realized that if I placed my hand just under the waterline, I wouldn't disturb their scramble to safety. As I snuck more glances at the branches close to us, I noticed everything from squirrels, to mice, and even snakes hanging from or scrambling up the limbs. They ran side-by-side, neither prey nor predators, as if a temporary truce had been called during the emergency.

As we entered the bottom of a meadow, we came around a gentle curve and could see the other road ahead. I began to wonder where we would land when I saw Sug begin to shove away from the log. What was he doing?

"The whirlpool!" he shouted and snapped his head in the downstream direction. Sug dove under the log and came up on the other side, swimming toward a tree with a dual trunk at the edge of the water. Oh, my God! I had forgotten about the whirlpool.

Panic set in as I ducked under the log and swam as hard as I could. Sug was a strong swimmer thanks in large part to his muscular build. I was rail-thin, and my form was more thrash than a stroke. I could feel myself being pulled past the tree, and I redoubled my efforts to make headway as the roar of vortex rose off to my right. I saw Sug grab onto the tree, but it felt as if I was losing ground in my attempt. My arms were hurting, and my lungs felt as if they would burst

All I could think of was that my parents were less than two hours into an eight-hour drive. What would they do if I killed myself two hours after being left alone for the first time? My mother would be so hurt. How could I have been so stupid?

"Help!" I managed to squawk as I caught a slight ripple in the water less than five feet away from me. In the periphery of my vision, I followed the line in the water to see a strand of barbed wire rise from the creek. Then I remembered there was a barbed-wire fence just before where the vortex was located. My mind exploded with visions of being tangled in barbed wire, being pulled under and ripped apart by the whirlpool. What a horrible way to die. Even if the vortex didn't get me, the current would hold me against the fence and drown me before anyone could get to me.

The exhaustion I felt in my arms was almost overwhelming. A part of me wondered what would happen if I gave in to the current. It was then that I saw Sug, wrap his left arm around the tree, and extend back to reach for me. We were feet apart now, but my arms felt heavy and slow. A final kick and I dipped my face into the water to lunge as far forward as I could. I was spent. I was desperate, and I was scared. I wondered if I would ever breathe again. I felt his hand wrap around my wrist. Too weak to move, I felt him pull me in, and I wrapped my legs around the tree, arms limp at my sides. We both clung there, trying to catch our breath. I looked back as the log slowly scraped past the barbed wire fence. As it travelled toward the vortex, the leading end of the log was pulled down into it so that the other end stood out of the water, twirling like a cocktail stick in a stirred drink.

Finally, between gasps for air, I heard, "Go again?"

"Not on your life."

Chapter 42
Fight with Neighbor

Most of the neighbors in the trailer park had long ago learned of my father's drinking and shenanigans, so they chose to keep a friendly distance. They preferred to just wave on the way to and from the car but not to engage him. The owner had expanded the number of lots after we live there a while. We now had neighbors on both sides, with an additional five or so beyond. The park had minimal turnover, so we became acquainted with everyone. The lot beside us when we moved in held a mother, father, and their one child, that was just a baby. The man was a nice, quiet guy who didn't drink and had little to do with my father. They moved out after about five or six years, and an older couple moved in. The man was small and wiry and reminded me of a bantam rooster who would strut around his yard with his shirt off. He had been in the navy and had a couple of tattoos, usually restricted to service men and bikers then. He was only about five foot five and probably a hundred and thirty pounds.

I can't remember his name, so I will call him Mister Snyder. I don't think he drank much, but I saw him with a beer now and then as he puttered around the yard or messed with his car. He and my father didn't interact much, so I was surprised to see the neighbor sitting in our house drinking a beer with my father one Saturday. Given his personality I had witnessed so far, I didn't think this would be a good mix. They drank some beer my father kept around for others or if he was working in the heat. By late afternoon they had switched to my father's usual bourbon and water, getting louder by the minute, telling stories and lies to one another.

I didn't stick around much, but when I came home toward dark, things had turned a corner between them. I found them standing out in front of my father's truck, having a heated discussion about something. They argued about the parking space where my father always kept his truck. The other trailer lot had a long curb on the side of it where the previous tenants had always parked. This new guy had gotten in his head that it must be his spot since it was closer to the front of his trailer than ours. I stood at our screen door and watched them, just in case.

It didn't take long until they decided to kick each other's asses. The shoving and name-calling started, so I went out to keep them separated. I didn't want to get kicked out of the park when someone called the cops. I managed to talk my father into going inside the house to cool off. I told Mr. Snyder to get into his place before somebody called the cops. He retreated to his sidewalk but stood there yelling insults and threats.

Meanwhile, inside, my father had done the most logical thing he could think of and went to bolster his courage with another drink, maybe two, I'm not sure. When he returned to the living room, he could hear the little rooster yelling from his sidewalk, and my father went out the door. I managed to get in front of him and stop him before he was halfway down the sidewalk, gradually coaxing him back while they threw insults back and forth. I finally got him back inside, with help from my mom, and I closed the front door, so he could not hear the neighbor.

When I turned around, the neighbor was on our sidewalk, his

courage braced by my father's retreat. At this point, I was losing my patience. It was bad enough dealing with one drunk, and now I had two on my hands. I marched to within a few feet of the neighbor and told him that if he didn't go inside, I would kick his ass. To my surprise, he turned and went home.

As I turned to go back in, I saw my father open the door and start onto the front step. Running to intercept him, I said, "No, you don't," shoved him inside, and closed the front door again. My father pushed against the door, but I was able to keep him from opening it. Then I heard his drunken footsteps plodding through the trailer, trying to reach the back door.

I ran to the back, getting there before he could get it unlocked and completely open. I threw my shoulder into the bottom of the door, preventing him from escaping. The door was three steps up, and I was at the bottom of the short metal staircase.

Changing direction again, my father stomped toward the front door. I raced to catch him, not realizing that he had doubled back. When I returned to the rear door, he had it open and was on the middle stair. Shit! I was so mad at the ridiculousness of the situation, at dealing with two drunks, and that one of them had just outsmarted me that I grabbed my father by his right leg and by the shirt. I picked him up and carried him up the final two stairs, into the bedroom, and threw him on top of my parent's bed. I was running on pure adrenaline. I stood there, pointed at my father, who lay stunned on the bed, and said, "If you get up again, I'm gonna knock you out." I walked out and slammed the door closed to ensure that the other drunk was still gone. When I entered the front door, I saw my father sitting at the foot of the bed.

Unknown to me, the neighbor's family who lived on the other side of us was watching this whole circus. He and his wife were in their early forties, with two girls, eleven and thirteen. His wife told him, "You should help that poor boy," his oldest daughter told me the next time she saw me.

Not wanting to get involved in a neighborhood dispute, he reluctantly went out and, as he rounded the corner of our trailer, witnessed me carrying my father up the steps and throwing him on the bed. He turned around and went home, telling his wife, "He doesn't need any help."

Chapter 43
Fight with Aunt Buster

My mom was the oldest in her family. She had two sisters, one named Wilda, whom everyone called Buster, and the youngest named Imogene, who everyone called Jean. When we lived in the second trailer park in New Jersey, my mom babysat Aunt Buster's youngest child, my cousin Jeff. She also had a daughter in junior high at the time, but since Jeff didn't go to school yet, and since they lived right across the bridge in Delaware, my mom watched him, and he was part of our family during the weekdays.

Buster was my favorite aunt when I was a kid for two reasons. First, whenever she came over, she always brought me a box of Cracker Jacks, the way to a young boy's heart. Buster always brought treats for the other kids, but I loved Cracker Jacks. The second reason is that she had a job and her own car. It was a sixty-one Oldsmobile, and I thought it was so cool. I wished that my mom had a car and a job like her. It never occurred to me that it would take her away from being home for us, but it worked in my young brain.

Because of my father's drinking, we didn't visit or do things with my other aunts and uncles often, even though they all lived within thirty minutes of us. But occasionally, there would be get-togethers which I always enjoyed if my father didn't cause problems. I enjoyed playing with all my cousins and thought my uncles and aunts were fun. My uncle Dick, mom's youngest brother, was always joking and teasing everyone. Buster's husband, Uncle Charlie, was more reserved but told good stories that I enjoyed. He had a subtle humor. Aunt Jean and her husband, Uncle Joe were also fun. He liked to tell jokes, and she had a great laugh you could hear often. You could tell my Aunt Jean was a real softie inside with an expressive face. I liked my mom's side of the family.

Much of the drop in number of get-togethers was my father's fault. Some of it was because the kids were growing and getting involved in things that made scheduling gatherings more challenging. The other cousins were especially busy with things like baseball. It seemed as we got older, we saw them less.

In high school, I remember Aunt Buster and her daughter, Linda, visiting. It was a Sunday, and they stayed for dinner, which surprised me. My father always liked Buster and the afternoon went pretty well. Of course, as the day progressed, my father drank more, but he seemed in a decent mood.

Linda was tall like my uncle, with dark hair that she wore in a 1960s flip and cat eyeglasses. She always seemed intelligent but shy and soft-spoken. I remember being stunned when Linda told my father he had always been her favorite uncle because he was funny.

It was summer and just getting dark when the mood suddenly turned for the evening. I don't remember why, but my father started degrading my mother. I think, at first, he was trying to be funny, but it didn't go over well with her sister. Buster said, "Now, Red, I don't want to hear that kind of talk about Marge."

That was it, and he started in on my mom and her sister, calling my mom fat and lazy and telling Buster if she didn't like it, she could get out of his house. Aunt Buster had always been somewhat more reserved, so I was sure she would start crying and leave. Instead, soon, she was standing face-to-face with my father telling him what she thought of him and how he treated her sister. Even more surprising, Linda was right behind her giving him hell too, taking back what she said about him being her favorite and now how she hated him.

My father was standing there red-faced and yelling back at her, just inches away, when to my surprise and disgust, he spat in my aunt's face. I couldn't believe what a low-life, loathsome thing he would stoop to doing. The next thing I knew, Buster slapped him, then spit back in his face. It may have snapped my father out of his anger, or perhaps it was now being faced with three irate women all in his face, screaming at him. He spun and quickly retreated to the bathroom, slamming the door.

My mother apologized to my aunt, more embarrassed than I'd ever seen her. I was also apologizing to both of them. They were gracious enough not blaming us and sympathized with what we dealt with regularly. Linda said she had heard stories about his behavior but could never believe them until now. They tried to talk my mother into leaving with them, but she declined. When they left, my mother sat in her recliner and cried tears of embarrassment and rage over the events.

I expected my father to come charging out of the bathroom, raging about my mom and her family. After a prolonged period of quiet, we peeked in the door to find him passed out in my parent's bed. My mom closed the bedroom door and slept on the couch that night. The next evening when my father came home from work, had his drink, and lay on the sofa, my mother let him have it in a stern calm voice, telling him how much he had embarrassed her, what her sister and her daughter now thought of him, and that she hoped he was proud of himself. His face turned red, but he said nothing.

Chapter 44
Catcall

My sister Annette struggled with weight for most of her adult life. She was never huge but bounced between gaining and losing in cycles. When she was first married, my sister was probably a few pounds over what she preferred, and she began working with her doctor to try to reach her target. A year or so later, she and Fred moved out of the apartment in town and purchased a trailer that became available in the trailer park where we lived. They didn't plan on living there forever but considered it a decent starter option.

Annette was on shift work at the same cardboard container plant where my Aunt Buster worked just over the Delaware bridge. She would rotate to a different weekly shift making a brutal schedule. I think the diet pills also helped her function, given that her schedule was constantly changing, and Annette seemed to shed some pounds, getting close to her target weight. I noticed she did not stay at that level for long but resumed gaining and losing that extra ten or fifteen pounds, just enough to bother her self-image.

I wondered in passing if she just got tired of dieting or had a more difficult time when the medical profession finally started steering away from handing out diet pills like candy. She might have learned to accept her body as it was, but she seemed to settle into a reasonably consistent weight that included those extra pounds. Fred didn't seem to hassle her about it and his weight even bounced around. I would remain pretty thin well into my forties before I started "filling out," as my mom called it, so I paid little attention.

Annette and I did not see each other as much when I was in my twenties because she and my first wife did not mix well. She thought my wife was a snob, and my wife considered her too sensitive. After my divorce, Annette and I became much closer, and one day, we were looking at some pictures. She handed me a photo of her in shorts at her thinnest. She said, "This was when I was right at my ideal weight."

I noticed that she suddenly got quiet. When I looked over, she had tears in her eyes. I wondered what had triggered them but wasn't sure how to approach such a sensitive subject.

"Wasn't that when you were on the diet pills? Those things weren't the best thing for you, you know." I tried to provide an out for her to use.

"I know." She sighed and, after a beat, said, "But that's not what caused me to gain the weight back."

"No?"

"You know what made me stop working so hard to get skinny?" Her voice broke as she said it.

"What was it?" I asked as I put down the pictures, giving her my full attention.

"Well, I was walking home from Edie's (the trailer park owner) one evening. It was a weekend. I wore these shorts to show Edie how much weight I'd lost." She choked up for a second. "She was really proud of me."

"That's good, right?"

"I was on my way back to mine and Fred's trailer, up by Curt's (another tenant,) and this car pulls up beside me and honks the horn.

Infertile Ground

I saw it was Dad's car out of the corner of my eye, so I thought he was just gonna say hello." She stopped again and grabbed a tissue.

"Anyway, he rolled down the window on my side, and I guess he didn't recognize me 'cause it was getting dark." She wiped a few tears. "And I heard this wolf whistle, and he said something to me."

"Maybe he was just kidding around."

"Oh, no. You don't say something like this to your own daughter, ever!" Her voice cracked again as she emphasized the last word. Tears flowed as she recalled the crude insult.

"Did you say something to him?"

"No. I just hid my face in my hands and ran across the backway through the yards to home."

"Did you tell Fred?"

"No. No. Fred would have gone over there and killed him. I couldn't tell Fred."

"I'm so sorry, Annette." I put my hand on her shoulder. What else could I say?

"And ever since then, whenever I started getting close to that weight or even thought about losing weight...remembering what he said to me...his own daughter. I just couldn't."

I sat with her while she cried, thinking what a bastard he was.

Chapter 45
Protecting the Corn

As kids, in the summer, we spent a lot of time in the woods, where we built log cabins and tree forts. We occasionally used these for camping out overnight. It was a way to gain freedom and spend time with friends. We would leave the house with some matches, a salt shaker, and maybe a blanket or beach towel for sleeping. The summer nights in New Jersey were often humid and sticky, so we'd slather on mosquito repellant or take a long-sleeved shirt. The uniform of our group was always no shoes, jeans, and a t-shirt (preferably army green). Occasionally sneakers were worn, but we were more likely to be barefoot.

We were free to roam around the area fields and roads on our bikes but hardly ever went more than a mile or two astray. We ventured out after dark in search of tomatoes, corn, or the best prize, watermelon, depending on the season. These were why we brought the salt shaker. Then we'd return to our camp and start a fire, standing in the smoke to help ward off mosquitos.

We would spend the evenings riding our bikes under the few street lights or shooting soda cans out of the corn gun to see whose projectile went farthest. The Jennings family used a corn gun (or bird cannon) to keep the birds out of the corn. Corn guns usually use propane. They make a loud bang every so often to scare the birds. They have a long tube that acts as a barrel, and we used the compressed air from the explosions to shoot projectiles. It was all harmless antics of kids that lived in the country.

The Jennings boys had an uncle who owned a construction company and decided to buy some of the land around their property. Part of it contained a blueberry field, and on another ten acres, the family planted corn. Not long after my brother had left for the Marines, we decided that we were going to camp out in that cornfield. We used the excuse of protecting the field from any would-be corn thieves. So off we went into the middle of the field to make camp. My mom and dad came home from grocery shopping to find the following note on the dining room table.

> Dear Mom and Dad,
> I've run away. Don't try to look for me 'cause I've changed my name, and I am staying in a corn field. Please don't cry, I may be back tomorrow (say around breakfast time.)
>
> Mike

I was surprised that Hawky's brother, Sug, had brought a twelve-gauge shotgun and a twenty-two-caliber pistol. He was serious. Then he told us that someone had stolen some corn a night or two before and that we would just use the guns to scare off anyone that didn't

Infertile Ground

leave when we told them. I didn't think we would encounter anyone, so I wasn't worried, especially since we would have a campfire in the middle of the field that they would likely see.

We settled in for the night, sitting around the fire and eating a few ears of corn, when we heard a car stop at the end of the field. Sug grabbed the shotgun and handed me the pistol. As we reached the end of the cornfield, we heard people speaking Spanish. Some kind of Hispanic music was loudly playing on the car's radio. They were likely migrant Puerto Rican farm workers, and there were at least five of them. "Let's split up. You two go to the right, and I'll go to the left."

"How will I know what to do?" I asked.

"Just follow my lead. If they are stealing, I'll yell to you. Otherwise, stay in the edge of the field where they can't see you."

We watched Sug disappear between the cornstalks, then went to where we could see the intruders, but we still hid behind the stalks. They were talking a mile a minute and standing right at the edge of the corn. They had an older two-door American car, and the passenger door was open. Since we didn't speak Spanish, we had no idea what they were saying. Hawky and I were nervous about being outnumbered by a group of men.

"Are they stealing? What should we do?" Hawky, under thirteen and unarmed, didn't like the odds.

"Do you see Sug?" I shrugged and listened intently.

"No."

Suddenly, I could hear Sug yell, "Mike, they are...." I didn't catch the rest of it because they all turned toward Sug's voice and began talking to each other excitedly. I looked back at Hawky, who just shook his head to indicate he hadn't caught it either. I didn't want to leave Sug exposed by himself, so I had to do something. I remember looking up at the starry sky, taking a deep breath, then stepping out of the field. I could still feel the rasp of the cornstalk leaves on my forearm as I stepped clear of the row. Raising the pistol, I fired a shot to let them know we had surrounded them.

All eyes of the group swung to me as the gunshot echoed against the woods in the distance. The excited chatter turned to shrieks as they scrambled toward the car, pulling at each other, trying to be first to get in. The only expression I could understand was "andele" from the Speedy Gonzalez cartoons. I heard the car start, the engine roared, and the back tires squalled as they gained purchase from dirt to asphalt.

Sug trotted toward me, yelling, "What the hell are you doing?"

As the taillights disappeared in the night, I told him, "I couldn't hear what you said. I thought you said they were stealing, so I had to do something."

"I said they were just taking a piss."

"I couldn't hear because they started yelling as soon as they heard you."

He started laughing. "They were just a bunch of drunk Puerto Ricans coming back from a night of drinking, and they stopped to take a leak. Then you come out shooting. They were probably pissing all over themselves getting back to the car."

"Well, at least they won't be back to steal corn." We were all laughing at the absurdness of the situation.

Sug stood on his toes to look over the corn, "We better get back and act like we're asleep in case the old man heard it and comes down to check." We sprinted back, laid down by the fire, and tried to control our fits of snickering.

Chapter 46
Educated Fool

I spent most weeknight evenings in the back room of the trailer, my parent's bedroom, doing my homework. At least, that was the excuse I used to get some privacy. I did do my homework, but I also wrote stories and poetry. Occasionally, I would quietly talk on the phone with my friends, although phone usage, while not prohibited, was discouraged. "Don't be tying up the line. Someone might call about something important," was the usual reason given.

It did cause me to focus on my studies, though, and as a result, my grades were good. As I entered my senior year, my friends were applying to schools and visiting colleges to decide on their choice. If it hadn't been for my guidance counselor, Mr. Robbins, I would never have completed the application process. I almost didn't anyway when I had to ask my father to provide income information to apply for financial aid and some scholarships. He did so reluctantly. Knowing I had no financial backing from my father, I mostly applied to state schools so that tuition would be lower.

During the college application process, the mystery of the gap between my oldest sister and my youngest sister grew in my mind. I needed to find my birth certificate as part of the submission. I was helping my mother look through the folder of important documents she kept when I found the children's birth certificates. As I leafed through them, I looked at the tiny footprints, amazed we were ever that small. I noticed that on one of them, I think it was my brother's because his was from South Carolina, there was an interesting entry. One line listed if there were any stillbirths, and they entered the number two in the field. I had never heard anyone talk about my mother losing any babies. Knowing it would be a difficult subject to discuss, and given my family's penchant for avoiding such discussions, I didn't ask my mom about it but stored it away mentally.

I applied to Stockton, Glassboro, and Rutgers. Carnegie-Mellon and a few other private schools actively recruited me, but when I compared the cost to the financial package they offered, I could not afford them. I was accepted at all the state schools but had to go with the one offering the most assistance, Glassboro State. Known as a teacher's college, it was not my preference, but my counselor had managed to get me into a program called the Martin Luther King Scholarship. It targeted poor minority students who were financially and academically challenged. "I am white and not academically challenged," I told my counselor. He just winked at me and said, "You'll be one of their success stories that will help the program get more funding." The catch was I had to attend preparation classes that summer to help me get up to speed for the fall semester, but I would get through college with almost no debt. Sold! I accepted the Glassboro offer.

I proudly told my parents my decision and how it wouldn't cost them anything. My mom was happy and proud of me. I also noticed an immediate change in my father's attitude toward me. I should have expected it but was surprised when the very next weekend, he directed his drunken rant at me.

"You think you're a big man now. Big college man, huh? You'll never be anything but an educated fool. I don't care what you learn there, boy; you'll never amount to anything. Book smart don't mean anything in the real world. You'll still be as stupid as you are now."

Infertile Ground

I was so happy to have been accepted and found a way to pay for it that I didn't care. "Sure. Whatever you say," I answered.

"You think you're gonna go to some fancy college, and get you some nice, rich college pussy, boy? Is that what you hope? Well, ain't no woman ever gonna want you. You're too damned ugly and stupid. What woman in her right mind would want a scrawny-assed little fucker like you? None. You couldn't keep a woman if you tried."

His insults went a little overboard, but I shook my head and walked away. I had a way out now, a path forward. He began to matter less and less, and I think he could see it because his verbal attacks and insults became angrier and more frequent. He seemed determined to pound that message into my brain and became more frantic as my time to leave drew close. The educated fool insult was the most frequent, though he would add comparisons to officers in the Army or idiot engineers he had seen specify things to be done that could never work or would have killed someone. "Was that what I wanted to be? Someone that people laughed at behind their backs?"

He did slip once when he was on a crying drunk, as my mom called it. He admitted wanting to be a writer if he could be anything. I was surprised at this since I had not seen him read a lot, perhaps a Readers Digest now and then. He hinted that he wanted to tell about his experiences in the war and some of his other adventures, like the time he crashed a plane. So, I knew he was jealous and threatened by me since I had opportunities never open to him.

It didn't mean it hurt less to have your father stand before you, telling you you're worthless, ugly, and would never amount to anything. It made it so that I entered that world feeling even more like I didn't belong and that soon they would see through me and know I was an imposter. I would continually be amazed later at those people around me in school and work that were ambitious and had a clear idea of what they wanted to do or what direction the world should take. I marveled at the idea they presumed to know such a thing. It is hard to feel sure about anything when your foundation is built on insult, abuse, and doubt.

Chapter 47

Graduation

When graduation finally came, I was still seventeen. My oldest sister had helped me find a car I could afford along with insurance a few months before. It was a three-hundred-fifty-dollar 1963 Buick Special, and I was thrilled to have it. It represented independence and freedom to me.

I expected little in the way of any celebration regarding my graduation. My parents attended the ceremony held in the gymnasium of our school. To my surprise, my mother arranged a party for me that weekend and invited all her family, aunts, uncles and cousins from Delaware. I would be one of the first in my family to go to college, the first in my immediate family. I felt a bit bad since none of my other siblings had a graduation party, but I was glad for any excuse to see everyone on my mom's side of the family. As always, there was an impending feeling of doom regarding how my father would act and whether he would use this chance to embarrass me and the rest of us.

It was a modest affair, held at our home, spilling into the front yard since it was a warm June evening. My father was even well-behaved, and the evening settled into a nice rhythm with my aunts and uncles sitting in lawn chairs in a circle on the front lawn. My Uncle Dick and Uncle Joe told jokes and stories while my Aunt Jean's cackle could be heard regularly. I drifted between chatting with my cousins who came and the adults while being congratulated and teased about being a college kid. It was a bit overwhelming since I had never been the center of attention for this group before, and my parents regularly told us that when the adults got together, children were to be seen and not heard. I was awkwardly stepping into the adult world.

My family was never the type to give high praise or show affection. I was more likely to get an affectionate slap on the arm from my mom than a hug. So, I was deeply touched when my Aunt Jean called me over in front of the whole group, handed me a card, and began saying how proud they were of me and how I should be proud of what I accomplished. The card had some money in it. I don't remember how much, because it didn't matter compared to the warmth that flowed over me as she praised me in public. She said she knew I would do well, something that terrified me as I stood on the threshold of the unknown. I remembered her gift of encouragement throughout my college years and vowed then and there to make them proud of me. Such a simple gift that sustained me countless times, lifting me in times of doubt.

I graduated near the top of my high school class and received several small scholarships from local businesses and organizations. One was a car dealer for whom I had worked washing cars in my senior year. I was shocked to hear my name called and see my name listed on the graduation program as the recipient. The award from the dealer was for five-hundred dollars which seemed like a lot of money at the time, and my mom brought out the program to show everyone.

My father drank little and remained quiet except for a few quips about me getting my brains from him. For a few minutes, I was foolish enough to think that perhaps he was impressed with my accomplishments and potential, my spirits riding high that evening. He dashed any such thoughts the next night as he listed the usual shortcomings, but they stung less that time.

Chapter 48

Construction Job

I had to report for the preparation classes in mid-July through August, so I had about a month to try to make some money. My oldest sister had moved back to the area, and her husband said he could get me a job helping on a construction crew doing some work in the DuPont plant where my father worked. It was good money, so I took it.

When I entered the plant, this vaunted world of my father, I was shocked. I knew it was a chemical manufacturing facility, but it seemed archaic. Open ditches flowed with chemicals that changed colors hourly, it seemed. Indeed, complex machinery and pipes flowed through impressive processes, but the crudeness of other parts seemed from the nineteenth century.

In all the company image advertisements, scientists were in clean white lab coats inside pristine laboratories. Here it was dirty buildings, ungodly smells, and warning signs everywhere. Our task was to dig out one of those flowing ditch cauldrons as the chemicals flowed through. I was a simple day laborer who stood by with a shovel as my brother-in-law used a backhoe to make the ditch deeper. He would bring up a bucketful of clay at a time, rainbow-colored by layers from all the dyes that had flowed through. The backhoe was to load them in a dump truck. I was there with a classmate who I recognized to catch drippings that fell short of the target. I cringed at the idea of getting any on me and did my best to stay clear of the mess. It reassured me of my choice of going to college because this didn't seem safe for man or the environment, and I wondered why they still did it this way.

We were short a man on my last day, so I was designated to drive the dump truck. While I took a truckload to the designated dump site, I later discovered my classmate slipped and fell into the ditch up to his waist. His skin was bright purple for weeks after that. I was sure that it would ruin his sex life if he had any, let alone any long-term effects.

Having put in my month there, I was both horrified and in admiration of my father's choice of employer. I feared what it had likely done to him working in such an environment, and I had to respect any man who would put himself in such personal peril to feed his family daily.

Chapter 49
Off to College

In mid-July, I left for the preparation phase of the scholarship deal. They told us it was also time used for them to evaluate us. I lived in a dorm for the summer, surrounded by students from all parts of the region. There were Chicanos from the tough parts of New York City whose brashness and false confidence were scary. Inner-city kids from Philadelphia and Newark, New Jersey, seemed wary and uncomfortable way out in the wilds of South Jersey. I made a few friends, a Puerto Rican mixed blood cross country star that would become my roommate during my first and second years and a girl from Bayonne on whom I would develop my first college crush. Unfortunately, she dubbed me a friend early in the relationship, and I never managed to change that evaluation.

The summer classes were things I had already learned but were a great review, especially the math, to prepare me for the fall semester. The friendships would also make the transition to college a little easier adjustment. My friend Dave (the cross-country star) and I found a room in a house off-campus together since we were too late to get rooms in the dorms. I remember signing the lease on the night that President Nixon resigned.

We would eat meals together in the cafeteria, and he, being a gregarious type, would introduce me to his many other friends. The scholarship paid for tuition, our meal tickets, books and provided money for rent. The room in town was cheap, and I was careful to follow a tight budget. I was also assigned a job working in the library at the college. Annette's husband was the manager of a fast-food restaurant and arranged for me to work there on the weekends to make money. After my first semester, I learned not to schedule classes on Friday so I could go home and work in the restaurant Thursday, Friday, and Saturday evenings. On Sunday mornings, I would go in before opening and scrub the patio (dining area) floor, then head back to school Sunday. This schedule allowed me to get close to thirty hours a week. Between the jobs, going to class, and doing homework, I had little to no time for a social life during college, which is a part I never experienced. But I made it through my freshman year, making mostly A's and some B's and hustling to make money.

Chapter 50
My House

I came home for summer vacation, looking forward to having some time to relax. I hoped to get more hours at the fast-food place to save money for the next semester. Even though the Martin Luther King scholarship covered most of my expenses, it didn't leave a lot for any extras, and I had car insurance and gas to get around, as well as clothes and miscellaneous expenses.

Because I had my car, I spent some time visiting with other friends who were home from college and comparing notes. They all seemed to be having a much better time at school than I was since I could never hit the social scene.

I enjoyed sleeping in late, relaxing in the afternoon, and then I would go to work. My schedule at work was about the same, mostly on weekends. My brother-in-law couldn't give me many more hours consistently, or the company would classify me as full-time, which would be a hassle for him, but he gave me what he could.

The first week seemed to go by quickly, and I worked my usual routine on Thursday, Friday, and Saturday. I would start at four in the afternoon and close, which meant we would stay after the store closed to clean and prepare the place for the morning shift. The business closed at midnight, so it was usually one o'clock in the morning by the time we finished cleaning. I made it home around one-thirty and crashed. I got up at seven, so I could go in and clean the patio Sunday morning. Since the place opened at eleven, I usually stayed and had something for lunch, then went home.

I was tired from little sleep the night before when I arrived home. As usual, I parked across the street, and as I approached our sidewalk, my father came out the front door heading toward his car. I tried not to make eye contact as I started past him, standing by his car door. I could tell by his eyes and his gait that he had a few drinks already and I did an inward eye-roll knowing the chances of me taking a nap would be nil unless he left.

"You got in a little late last night." I heard as soon as my back was to him.

"Excuse me?"

"I said you got in a little late last night. I want you in here by midnight."

I couldn't believe it. "Look, I was working."

"When you're away at college, you might pull that shit. But I said you need to be home by midnight."

"Hey, if I was out screwing around, I can see it. But since you're not paying for my school, I have to work to save money."

Out comes the old nugget I'd heard all my life. "It's my house. When you live under my roof, you live by my rules."

I stood there looking at him in disbelief. It had nothing to do with fairness, and he had no sympathy for my situation. I was tired physically and tired mentally of his crap. I had experienced a taste of freedom, living on my own for the past year at school. It would be difficult, but I knew I could make it. I could stay with my sister for the summer months, or if that didn't work, I still had the room in Glassboro through August. It would be a long commute, but I could do it if necessary.

"Fine," I said. I walked into the house and packed what I had brought home from school. My mom asked me what I was doing.

"Moving out," I said. Then I told her about the exchange outside. I walked out the front door, followed by my mom, who was crying.

As I walked past him toward my car carrying my stuff, he said, "Hey boy, get your ass back here. I'm not done talking to you."

I heard my mom start in on him to leave me alone, but I stopped and turned around. They both looked over toward me as I looked him straight in the eyes and said something I had always wanted to say my entire life, "Fuck you, old man." And I turned around and left.

I could see his mouth moving as I turned my car around, but I had turned the radio up full blast and pulled away. My sister only lived a short distance from where I was parked, but I figured I'd go back to work and talk to Fred, my brother-in-law, first. I stayed in my sister's spare bedroom that first night. After that, a new guest occupied it, my mother, who moved out the next day. We stayed with my sister. My father was afraid of my brother-in-law because Fred was big, but mostly because my father knew he would call the police, so he didn't try to bother us there.

After a month or so, my mom found a tiny house that she could afford with two bedrooms, and we moved in. She worked hard with the help of my sister and applied for all the assistance she could get and found a job cleaning office buildings with a family friend. She never returned and divorced him when she could afford to do so a few years later.

Money was always a struggle. I helped where I could, and in her early fifties she had to learn how to open a checking account and pay bills for the first time in her life. A friend of mine gave her a car that needed some work, and fortunately, after some minor repairs, it lasted her quite a few years. She was free and much happier than I had seen her in a long time.

This story is as much my mom's as mine. Without her strength, I would never have made it. She divorced my father in her mid-fifties and did eventually remarry. Her husband would not have been my first choice as I had hoped for a retired teacher similar to Mr. Sorrels for her. This time she was the boss, handled the money, and married a man younger, almost the same age as my oldest sister. He was nice to her, though he did drink. I don't know if she managed to work out all the damage my father had done, but she certainly learned to control her world. She died shortly after her eightieth birthday of a stroke in 2004. My oldest sister died of kidney cancer in 2001. My mother never got over it before she passed. My brother died of lung cancer in 2011, and my youngest sister died of uterine cancer in 2019.

Chapter 51

Open Question Answered

In the early fall, after my mother and I moved out, back in 1975, we decided to visit my Aunt Jean. My aunt lived in Delaware, and I always enjoyed seeing her. I remember sitting in her dining room, where she served us coffee, tea, cake, and cookies. She lived in a small but well-appointed home. It felt cozy and safe sitting, listening to my mom and aunt talk about family and how things were going. I remember thinking this was how I wanted my life to be. I didn't need a large house or many things, just a safe, welcoming home where I could control who was in my life. As I had many times, I promised myself I would make it true one day. I would welcome my mom's side of the family. I always enjoyed my time with her siblings and my cousins and hoped that I would be able to see them more frequently than had been possible with my father's drinking hanging over our heads.

"What's going on with Red?" my aunt asked at one point. "Do you think you all will get divorced?"

"I don't know yet. But I should have divorced the son-of-a-bitch a long time ago." My mom said, and despite the anger in her voice, she burst into tears.

It took me off guard. I had expected the anger, but the tears were something else. Was she sad about her thirty-plus-year marriage ending? Did she suddenly realize she loved him despite all the horrible things I had witnessed him do to her? My aunt was also concerned and told her that it was okay. They didn't need to talk about it now if she didn't want.

Tears flowed down my mother's face, but I could also see her struggling to compose herself. She took a few gulps of air, then seemed to steel herself and continued.

"I've never told anyone this before." She looked at Aunt Jean. "You remember that time I miscarried before Annette was born? When we still lived in West Virginia?"

Jean looked at my mom with a look of concern building on her face. "Did he do that? Did Red hit you or something that caused it?"

My mom took a few gulps of air, and then the tears started again. "I was almost seven months pregnant. He came home drunk from one of his overnight binges back then. I had no idea where he was, and we didn't have any groceries in the house, so I called Shorty, (my father's dad), who had brought us milk, eggs, and a few other things from the store." She stopped and closed her eyes, breathing deeply, reconstructing the scene in her head.

"Marge, you don't have to...." Jean reached over and put her hand on mom's shaking hand.

"No," a few gulps more. "The son-of-a-bitch was calling me everything in the book, right there in front of his father, and asked what the hell he was doing there. I tried to explain that Ritzie was hungry and we had nothing to eat. That his own father had to bring us food for his kid, whom he wasn't providing for, while he was out boozing it up and spending his money on his whores.

"Well, this set him off. He told Shorty to get his ass out of the house, then he turned to me and started mocking me, saying, 'my kids? My kids? I watched you running around in your little, short shorts, showing everything you've got to anyone who'll look. What I want to know is who's fucking kid this is?' pointing at her pregnant abdomen.

"At this point, I was standing in the bedroom doorway, and he began poking me in the belly, forcing me back toward the bed. I was terrified as he took the palm of his hand on my forehead and pushed me backward onto the bed. Being pregnant, I lay there struggling to get up as he ran to the kitchen and returned quickly, saying, "We'll take care of this little bastard right now."

My mom gasped for air but was determined to go on, and tears were streaming down my aunt's face. "When... when he came back in, he was carrying a bottle brush, and he grabbed me, pulled up my house dress, tore off my underpants, and shoved it up in me. I tried to kick him, but he was too strong, and I was shocked, hurting from the brush and screaming for him to stop. Shorty was in the bedroom doorway, yelling for him to stop. He finally let me go, and I rolled to my side, but I could tell I was bleeding, and the pain was intense."

She gasped a few more times, then continued, but her voice was much softer now, remembering the horror. "The baby came a few minutes later. Shorty helped me deliver it, then handed it to me. I just sat there crying and holding this perfectly formed little baby. It was tiny. I held it as it tried to breathe, but it couldn't because it was too young, and it died right there in my hands.

"I had heard Red's car leave. Shorty took the baby from me, and I never saw it again. I don't know where he buried it. I tried to clean myself up but was sore, crying, and angry."

"Oh my God, Marge," was all my aunt could manage to say. I had no idea what to do. So many emotions flooded through me at that moment. I wanted to hug my mom and tell her it was okay and she was finally free of him. I wanted to kill my father for this and all the horrible things he had done. I wanted to cry for my unborn sibling and somehow make up for such an awful end. I felt horror, knowing that I was flesh and blood of this monster. Did this mean I was capable of such things? Would people know? Could they tell that I had this in me? Was I doomed to be like him?

My mom continued. "I had left him once before. I felt so trapped. You just go into self-preservation mode, and later that day, when he came back, I could tell he was sorry. I know that Shorty gave him a strong talking-to, and threatened him, so he behaved himself for a long time after that. I was stupid enough to hope he had changed. But that's when I should have left him. That was when." You could see her chiding herself.

"You were just trying to take care of you and little Ritzie," Aunt Jean assured her. "You did what you thought best for her."

"And then I was pregnant with Annette not long after when he was acting better. Then Buddy and Mike came along."

There they were, the burden and the secret I took on right there. I never told anyone about this secret. I never told my sisters or brother because I didn't want them to carry this secret for the rest of their lives. I never told my friends, fearing their reaction and shame, that I came from such a man. I never told anyone until I wrote it here.

The burden was the guilt of being the youngest and knowing it was my fault that my mother had to be there longer because of me. She stayed because of the kids, and I had heard numerous times during arguments that she would have been long gone if it weren't for the kids. Every time he hit her, or I saw her black eye or bruise, I knew it was because of me that she was there. Whenever I saw tears falling, I knew that I had a hand in them.

I carried that burden for all my childhood until I finally stood up to him and, after a taste of freedom, knew there was no way I could keep doing it. So, I left, sure that I could make my way somehow. Even though I carried his voice in my head that I would be nothing, ever, but an educated fool that no one would love. I carried that secret for over forty years and am finally putting it down.

Leave it there. As I said, learn from it. Sure, you can study it, look at it. Tug at its heft to see what it might weigh, and you can even kick it or curse it, but leave it where it is.

I also took an oath that day. I had always promised myself I would try to not be like my father. This story made me swear to be his exact opposite. I would be nothing like him, the Ying to his Yang. If he did x, I would do y. I made a pact to be so vigilant that no one could ever accuse me of being like him. I would never hit a woman, no matter what she did. I knew if I ever did, I would self-destruct instantly in the realization that I had become what I hated most. I would finish college just to spite him. I would not drink alcohol. I promised myself repeatedly each time I thought of this tragic story. I became terrified that I had the slightest chance of becoming him. I had nightmares about it and woke up feeling I had to remain on a straight and narrow path because of this possible predisposition. It became all-consuming. Hard on myself for the slightest mistake, I knew I must be vigilant. Whatever I thought he would do, I would lean toward the opposite.

This rigid vigilance would eventually become crippling, and it would take me the rest of my life to unlearn it. Defining yourself as the opposite of someone is so confining that you can never be whole if you live your life that way. But to say this day was a defining moment in my life would be an understatement. To carry a dark secret, so consuming that healthy self-worth could never be possible.

Part Four

Adulthood

Chapter 52
Finish College and Go to Graduate School

For the next several years, my main focus was to finish college. My hectic schedule continued, taking jobs to pay for school and trying to help my mom. I was majoring in psychology, probably chosen to figure out why people do horrible things. I read for a woman who was legally blind and was related to my guidance counselor. I began to wonder about my choice when we visited a psychiatric hospital. I wasn't sure if I could deal with that environment daily. I watched my friends working on some of the helplines where people came in with problems and listened to their frustration at having worked with a person for months, only to have the person return to the behavior that started the process. I learned that a bachelor's in psychology likely limited you to being a social worker.

When I took an industrial psychology course, I knew it was much more to my liking. It was more scientific, and you would deal with more "normal" people. The professor spent one lecture railing about how the college was not preparing us for graduate school and the world. He had a consulting firm and was an adjunct professor. He read off some of the courses offered that seemed laughable. I approached him after class, explaining how I was a first-generation college student, and asked what I needed to do to graduate school. He asked about my grades (I was at a 3.6 out of 4). Those were okay but not outstanding. He asked about experience in the field, and I told him none and asked how could I get some.

"I have a project coming up where I could use you. You want a job?" I couldn't believe it.

"Yes, sir!" It was 1976 before the government approved halogen headlights in the US. The National Highway Safety Administration wanted a study done measuring the increase in glare from halogen headlights on the highway before they would approve them. So, I joined his small team along with a recent Master's graduate in human factors, and the professor. We spent our nights on a drag strip, using a car with racks on the front filled with lights. A target car had a photometer, and we did exhaustive testing from various distances and heights. The professor even included my name on the final report to NTSA. As a result of meeting the Masters graduate, I determined I also wanted to get a master's in human factors.

I had not seen or spoken to my father since our last encounter. My mother constantly worried he would find out where we lived the first year and harass us. Eventually, we heard that he had taken a medical retirement from DuPont, cashing in those chips from inventing the lathe, and moved back to West Virginia. He didn't come to my college graduation or even acknowledge it.

Just before graduation, I heard a student in class telling her friend that she was graduating cum laude. I assumed it had something to do with a sorority. She seemed excited and mentioned her grade average concerning it. I knew my grade average was pretty good, so I made a note to look into it. It turned out that cum laude meant she had a 3.5 grade point average. With my 3.71, I would graduate magna cum laude. The only thing higher was a summa cum laude at 3.95. I was graduating with honors.

I applied and was accepted at the same school where the Master student had gone, Stevens Institute of Technology in Hoboken, New Jersey. It was a private school and the cost was expensive, almost making me balk. Even with the financial aid they offered, I would have to take a loan for five thousand a year to cover the costs. I have to give credit to my girlfriend, who said, "If you needed a new car, you wouldn't think twice about taking a loan for five or ten thousand dollars. Why not do it for your future?"

Graduate school was a grind because I couldn't afford an apartment in Hoboken, across the river from Manhattan. So, I lived at home in south Jersey and commuted. It was about one hundred and ten miles each way. I would leave at seven in the morning to be at my on-campus job by nine. My job with another grad student was to run the student job program for undergraduates on campus. All the graduate classes were in the evenings for people that were working. So, I would go to class from six until nine, then jump in my car for the two-hour drive home. Living at home allowed me to help my mom some too. In my first year, I got all B's. The only time to read or do homework was weekends and sneaking time during work.

In the second year, I stayed with the graduate student from the headlight study. He had taken a job with AT&T and was living near Hoboken. I would sleep on his couch on Tuesday, Wednesday, and Thursday nights. In my final year, I got all A's, averaging a 3.5, and my Master's degree. AT&T people in my classes surrounded me. Bell Laboratories also sent many people to Stevens to get their Masters on a special program they had. I attended one class where even the professor worked at Bell Laboratories. They naturally asked where I planned to work as I got to know them. So again, through these connections, I ended up at Bell Laboratories. They prided themselves on only hiring the upper ten percent of graduates.

Again, my father did not attend or acknowledge my Master's graduation from Stevens. My mom and Annette attended. I had recently gotten married to the girlfriend who convinced me to take the loans. She, her mother, and her sister and brother also attended.

Chapter 53

Ex Sees Real Father

My father managed to briefly re-enter my life the following year. My wife took a job in Philadelphia, and after living with my mom for a year to pool resources, we rented a separate house not far away. My father had come up from West Virginia. I have no idea why and didn't care. He visited Annette and Buddy, who seemed to hope for some miracle father/child reunion, which I had given up long ago. He found out where I lived through them and decided to visit us. It was during the last semester of graduate school on a Saturday, so we had the misfortune of being home. My wife answered and let him in when he showed up at the door. I was okay with it because I could see that he had not been drinking yet, or at least not enough to start trouble. He sat on a chair by the front door. We sat on the couch. We exchanged a few attempts at pleasantries, and then he turned his attention to my wife, asking her about her work.

At one point, he asked me if I minded if he took a drink.

"Do you mean whiskey?" I asked.

"Bourbon," he corrected.

"We don't have any," my wife informed him, probably hoping it would end it.

"I have some in the car."

"I would prefer that you didn't drink in my house," I informed him.

"Okay. I'll be right back then." He got up and went out to his car.

"He doesn't seem so bad," my wife said when he was outside.

"Wait. It's just starting." He came back in with some color on his face, and the telltale blinking had started. He had probably done a double. Still, he seemed to maintain decorum for the most part though an opening salvo indicated the beginning of hostilities.

"I didn't think you would ever find such a pretty wife." My wife took the compliment at face value, but I knew more was coming.

Not long after, he took another walk to his car. I informed her that we needed to tell him we were leaving soon for something planned. When he entered, I could see that he had hit it pretty hard again, and I think even my wife could see the effect because she offered. "Can I get you some coffee or something?" She was hoping it would counter the alcohol.

"Sure," he said, "That would be great."

I walked into the kitchen as if to help her. "Don't bother. He just wants to be waited on at this point."

"I have to now. I offered" She made the coffee and set it beside him on the end table.

As soon as we sat down again, he said, "You know, I think you're too goddamned ugly to be my son."

"What do you mean? He looks just like you." My wife's fuse was lit. My father smiled at her, pleased he had gotten a reaction. She sat there fuming, her right eyelid at half-staff, indicating her disgust.

I decided to call it. Looking at my watch, I said, "Well, we need to get moving if we're making that thing." Then to my father, "Sorry, we have something planned this evening, so we'll have to leave here pretty quick."

I told her to grab her purse so we could make a show of going somewhere, and maybe a ride would help her cool off. To my surprise, my father took the hint. It only took another five minutes to get him out of the house. The coffee sat there, untouched.

Once we were in the car and sure he wasn't following, I asked, "So, how do you like the old man now?"

Chapter 54
Join Bell Labs

Two weeks after I graduated with my Master's degree, I joined Bell Telephone Laboratories. Because I entered the company with the help of my classmates who had become friends, I didn't realize what a big deal Bell Labs was as a world-class research organization. I liked it immediately because it felt like a continuation of graduate school. You called everyone by their first names, even levels above you. Continued learning was encouraged and even expected. I worked with some of the brightest people in every field of science and technology. I was somewhat intimidated. Most people had engineering or degrees in what they labeled the hard sciences, as opposed to the soft science of psychology.

I was sent off to training classes for the first month or so. When I went to my first meeting, it was a review of a requirements document for a new system. I spent the entire time writing down acronyms to look up later. I had no idea what they were talking about, but I could tell the engineers and software developers were tearing apart this document my group had prepared. I wrote on a small piece of paper and pushed over to a member of my group who had befriended me,

"Are all Bell Labs meetings like this?" He wrote something and discretely pushed it back. The note said, "Bell Labs eat their young!"

I had walked in the door of the place thinking. Here I am, this great slab of clay with unlimited potential, shape me to fulfill my destiny. My first supervisor was the type of guy who assumed you were an idiot until you proved him wrong. He was gruff and sarcastic, with little patience for teaching. His first assignment for me was to visit the people in the field to determine if the system they used needed any new features and to write the new requirements for any needed.

I spent three months visiting sites, and they all told me that the system already had so many features they didn't use half of them. I wrote my report. At review time, my manager told me I didn't do well because there were no new requirements for the system. After that, my assignments were junk work. This continued until I walked into his office and told him I wanted better assignments and that I was as good or better than anyone he had in his group. After watching the people around me, I realized I did not need to be intimidated. These people weren't smarter than me. They just had different interests.

I took a temporary assignment in a different organization as part of a plan for promotion to the next level. While there, the split of the Bell System hit in 1984. I had a choice of returning to my old group or staying with the new organization. I left my group to move to the part that became Network Systems, then Lucent. I could move around and gain experience in different parts of Lucent. At one point, I was given an honorary promotion to Distinguished Member of Technical Staff, which was only the top ten percent of the technical population then.

My job titles varied from Human Factors engineer to Market Manager during my tenure. I retired after twenty-eight years. The Bell Laboratories I joined does not even exist anymore. The splits and acquisitions have left it but a shadow of its former glory. We lost a national treasure. After a short four-year stint at a start-up in Oakland, California, I retired for good.

Chapter 55
Last Contact

My father ended up living in a thirty-foot camper trailer in his mother's backyard. His father had passed away years before from cancer. He was living on Social Security and the pension from DuPont and had not stopped drinking or smoking. My wife and I had gone to West Virginia and stopped by to visit his mother briefly, trying to avoid him, but we did see him a few times, usually resulting in awkward chats about his mother's garden or how my siblings were doing.

Once I started at Bell Labs, my wife and I had to decide on where to live since she worked in Philadelphia and I worked in Piscataway, NJ. We tried to find a middle ground and lived near Princeton for a couple of years. When we started looking for a house to buy, we ended up just inside the Pennsylvania border, but I had transferred to Holmdel, so I ended up with a ninety-minute commute.

After we had been there for about a year, my father found our phone number in my grandmother's address book near her phone. He called one Saturday and was cordial at first. He asked me, "Why did you never bother to call your old Dad."

I told him I didn't think we had all that much to discuss. As he became increasingly belligerent, I told him I was done talking to him. I said now that he had my number, he was welcome to call me anytime, when sober, but to please not call me when he was drinking. He began to call me names, so I hung up.

He rang back and cursed me when I picked up the phone. After the second time, I managed to interrupt him. I said, "If you pick up your phone book, look on page three (or whatever page it was in my book). You'll see that it is a felony to harass someone by phone. So, if you continue to call here yelling abuses, there will soon be a knock on your door from the police." I hung up the phone and never spoke to him again.

Chapter 56

Won't Bring You Supper

I got the call in September of 1986 that my father had died of a heart attack the night before. It was a strange feeling of both relief and loss at the same time. I struggled about going to the funeral since we had not parted on good terms, plus my wife and I were having some issues at the time. At least she was acting like a stranger to me. My siblings wanted me to go, so I agreed. I asked my wife, hoping for some support, but my wife declined, saying something about not wanting to witness the drama around my siblings. These same siblings rarely spoke of their emotions. Something didn't make sense to me.

So, I went with my sisters and brother. Most of my father's brothers and sisters beat us there, and my grandmother's house was full of people, which was good for her. We decided that my oldest sister would be in charge of handling things. A quick assessment determined that he owed more than his estate was worth, so there wasn't anything to divide except his personal items. He was given military honors with a twenty-one-gun salute by a rag-tag group of fellow VFW members that did their solemn best. He would receive a grave marker indicating his service. My sister later arranged for a headstone.

We spent several days going through his trailer. He had things squirreled in every nook and cranny. I wanted nothing of his personal effects. I was surprised to find he saved a few mementos relating to me. One was the note shared above informing my parents about my night to be spent in the cornfield. He kept an announcement cut from the paper of my college graduation. Another was a piece I had written as a preteen. Annette handed them to me, saying, "See, he was proud of his little boy," with tears in her eyes.

We were sitting in the trailer, going through mounds of worthless paper, old bills, magazines, and all the remnants of my father's existence when we heard the door open. My grandmother, my father's mom, came out to check how we were doing. My grandmother was a soft-spoken religious woman, frail in her late eighties. She was taller than my grandfather, at around five foot five, to his five two. She had survived cancer, and I'm convinced she had steel in her spine as strong as she seemed at times. Her vocabulary consisted of a lot of words that rang of folksy music. She would be fixin' to do something or eat a little dab of beans. I loved just sitting and talking with her, trying to memorize her expressions to treasure them.

As she stood holding the trailer door, refusing my offer of a seat, I looked down and noticed a bullet hole in the door. I casually asked, not expecting her to know, "I wonder what happened there?" pointing at the hole.

"Well," she started a lot of sentences this way drawing it out southern-style. "I had fixed me some supper and decided I would bring a little something out for Ernest." She always called my father by his Christian name. "So, I made him a little plate of beans and cornbread and whatever meat I had prepared. I knocked on the door, and he was sitting in that corner with the pistol in his hand." She indicated the recliner where my oldest sister was sitting. "I stepped inside and put the plate on the table and turned around about to go out the door holding on to the knob, and he shot right through the door there."

"Oh my God, Grandma, what did you do? You must have been scared to death." My sisters and I asked almost together.

"Well, I told him. Iff'n he was gonna shoot at me, I wouldn't bring him any supper no more, and I walked out."

I pictured this tall, thin, frail woman standing up to him, utterly unshaken by his antics. Despite the danger of what could have happened, I had to smile at this rock of a woman. "Well, good for you, Grandma. That's telling him."

I don't mean to imply that my father was the devil incarnate with my story. He was a severely damaged person from the war. He seemed to have been a sensitive kid from what I have heard. The war with everything he saw and did in it would be enough to change anyone. I know my brother also had his demons from what he witnessed in the evacuation of Saigon, including people throwing their babies to try to get them in the closing door of the helicopter and hearing them bounce off. I would not have come out of combat the same as a kid. My father's drinking was his way of coping because there was not the types of support available as now. Why he turned it against his family, I don't know, but that sensitive kid was gone when I came along. He was replaced by a wounded, crippled man suffering with alcoholism and uncontrolled anger. An anger that indiscriminately hurt everyone around him.

As a child I saw the anger and out of self-preservation determined to avoid him. As a young adult I sensed that until he fixed whatever the damage was, there would be no positive relationship possible, something my siblings all struggled to accept. It is sad that he never managed to find help. I think I could have been friends with that sensitive kid on the bus who cried when the egg he was taking home to his mother was broken. The boy who wanted to be a writer. But I never met him.

Chapter 57

More Bad News

I left West Virginia, thinking about my father's behavior. How he had pushed everyone away and died, drunk and alone. He died of a heart attack, and did make it to a hospital so not technically alone, but still living in his camper in his mother's yard. I was determined not to let that happen in my own life, so I sat down with my wife to work out what was wrong. As I mentioned earlier there had been a distance I felt between us for a few months. I assumed it was because I had balked at having a child earlier that year. I was not totally against it, but after close to ten years of my wife saying she didn't want kids and "punch that kid in the face" whenever she heard a baby cry in public. Suddenly, she wanted one. I assumed she was turning thirty, and the alarm clock had chimed. My response was not a hard no, but I said, "Let's think about this because you can't send them back."

So, I sat her on the couch and said, "if that's the problem, let's do this," expecting to go upstairs to start trying.

"I want a divorce," was the answer instead.

That was not even an option I had considered. After much crying, talking, and counseling, where she sat like a stranger and blamed everything on me, we did that. We separated. When it came out, after trying everything I could imagine to mend things, that she had started an affair six months before my father's death, I was done.

We started dating at 19, married at 23, and basically grew up together. I don't claim to be innocent because the rigidity and high standards I had imposed on myself spilled over onto those who didn't sign up for them to some degree. We divorced and between the two major life blows I entered a severe depression. The kind of depression where you wake up in the morning and think, "What's the point?" To survive you have to break things down to the level of, "Okay, all I have to do next is to put my socks on." Once that was done, you thought of what small task to do next because to think beyond that was too overwhelming. I was shattered.

The good news is that the depression that followed helped me find a counselor specializing in children of alcoholics. It put me on the road to healing.

Part Five

Road to Healing

I don't dare suppose myself expert enough to tell anyone what to do if they are in a similar situation. I just thought I'd offer a few things I have learned that helped me through the years. I'm unsure what gave me the strength or stubbornness to survive and overcome my childhood's toxic, abusive environment. I know having a mother who loved me was a big part. I wouldn't have survived without her. I can't claim to know the whole story of my siblings and would never compare myself to them. We all struggled and suffered to find our own way. Once out of the pressure cooker, I became much closer to them in adulthood. Even my brother and I, who fought continuously in childhood, grew much closer. I learned to admire him and the things he accomplished that I know I could never do, especially raising five kids. He earned metals in the Marine Corps for his service and was crew chief of a helicopter that flew the most hours during the evacuation of Saigon at the end of the Viet Nam War. He was chief of Marine II which flies the Vice President and other dignitaries around. What more could a man ask for but to be a hero to his fellow service men, and earn the devotion of his children.

    My sister, Annette, continued to be an organizer, and upon her death, I learned how many people she had helped in life. She was a quiet angel of mercy many times and a stubborn, immovable rock when she felt she needed to be. I miss her in more ways than I can count.

Rita, or Ritzie, was never given the opportunities I enjoyed. Some I created, others I stumbled upon. I am convinced my siblings had unique gifts that made them who they were. Rita had it the hardest, I think, in both childhood and all her life. Some by her choices, but many by circumstance.

From an early age, I promised myself repeatedly that I would MAKE my life different. The events like the confrontation of the black men on our sidewalk caused me to reject my father's values, allowing me to find my own. My focus on learning and education, thanks to people like Mr. Sorrels, my fourth-grade teacher, helped opportunities open for me. Men like my Grandfather Droddy and Mr. Sorrels helped shape my internal definition of how to be a man, and I searched for examples to follow where I could. Having the strength and people around me to support me, when I asked for help allowed me to find counselors who led me to cognitive behavioral therapy, which gave me tools to cope and to climb out of my depression.

My simple take on this area of psychology boils down to just a few things. You grow up learning from others, and the significant ones in your life have the most impact, good or bad. You learn to internalize their voices that you use to guide you.

An example: One of the loudest voices in my head was my father's. So as a kid, I had a very short temper. Whenever I made a mistake, I immediately started yelling at myself internally. "You IDIOT! How could you be so stupid!" I would get angry and fly off the handle. When other people did things I didn't like, I would share that voice with them and call them idiots. That wasn't doing anyone any good.

How to fix it: What I learned that works for me is that anytime I react with strong emotion to a situation, I taught myself to stop! Then ask, "Where is this coming from? How much has to do with the current situation versus how much is a voice from the past?" So, when I felt myself boiling over, I would say, "Wait, I'll be back in a bit." Then I would go try to answer those questions. Ninety-nine percent of the time, if I reacted strongly, it was because of some old voice in my head. It is not easy to figure out sometimes, but it's a skill you learn and improve. When you separate that ninety-nine percent from the past and deal with the one percent in front of you now, life becomes a lot easier. Nowadays, when I make a mistake, I am more likely to laugh and call myself silly. The same with other people. Calling them silly feels a whole lot less judgmental than calling them stupid.

That's a very simplified explanation of cognitive behavioral therapy. Look for a book called "Feeling Good" by David M. Burns (MD). There are many other parts, but that had the most significant impact on me. The other thing you will learn is that you have tremendous skills as a child of an alcoholic. The not-so-good news is that many of them don't work or can't be applied well in the real world.

Mismatched Skills for the Real World

Earlier I mentioned how quickly I needed to be able to read the mood of a room when I walked in. That skill can occasionally be valuable when entering a corporate meeting when things get dicey. Still, most of the time, it's an over-developed muscle that alcoholic families have.

A quick example of some things that I had to learn or relearn completely. Some were behaviors others did easily, but I didn't know how to do them. Others are behaviors that I made a conscious decision to unlearn.

Chapter 58

Things You Don't Know

Social Skills

Because of my father's behavior, my entire family avoided gatherings, going places, or bringing friends around our home. As a result, all that time hanging with other kids or going to restaurants where you observe other families, parties, and gatherings never happened. As a result, I felt uncomfortable at gatherings because I had no idea how to act. It becomes a self-perpetuating problem—simple things like which silverware to use when – were a mystery for me at my first corporate meetings. I had to wait to see what others did and copy them. Small talk used to baffle me, but now I can at least fake it. One valuable thing my mother taught me when I mentioned that I was nervous going into these fancy places and big meetings. She said, "When you feel nervous, you just walk in there like you own the place." The more modern version is 'fake it 'til you make it." It helped me get over my fear of gatherings and giving presentations.

What do you want?

Here's a simple question that baffled me as I entered adulthood. My friends or others might ask me. What would you like to do? Where do you want to eat?

I had no idea how even to begin to figure that out. I would look at them blankly or meekly say, "Whatever." All my life growing up, I had never been given a choice. I spent my entire existence trying not to be noticed so that I wasn't a target for abuse. All attention focused on my drunk father. No one else mattered. My opinion did not matter. I did not matter. I was trained to go along. I would do what my father dictated. There was no other choice. That idea, that muscle, if you will, had never been developed.

Suddenly, my friends, girlfriend and then my wife would become frustrated with me because I could not tell them what I wanted. I wasn't even sure how to start to find out. It took me years to feel confident enough and to occasionally put myself first.

Ambition

The inability to know what you want directly leads to direction and ambition issues. When you first go to college, they ask you what your major will be? I had no idea. I think I chose psychology to try to figure things out for myself. I was amazed at the kids around me that were driven by their goals. I wanted to do well and make the dean's list, but I had no idea what career path I would follow. When I met kids in college who would want to get a business degree, start their own company and be a millionaire by thirty, I figured their parents had mapped that all out for them. You end up handicapped from the start compared to kids with a plan.

As you can tell from this book, I knew I wanted to be like Mr. Sorrels and attend college. I made it with hard work and the help of my guidance counselor. I became a psychology major to determine why my father did what he did or why people generally do things.

After a professor said they weren't preparing us for grad school or a career, I approached him. That led me to meet the graduate student, which led me to Stevens. Then, everyone in graduate school was AT&T, which led to working at Bell Labs. I just went through life stumbling into things instead of with a plan. How much more I could have accomplished will never be known. I am not complaining because I had a good career and enjoyed everything. Besides being a rock star, I accomplished every life goal I set for myself, so I have no complaints. Still coming out of an alcoholic family, it is a handicap you must overcome.

Boundaries

In my family, you were not allowed to have boundaries, let alone define them to suit you. Again, since all the focus was on my father, and I was trying to be invisible, I never learned to say, "you can go this far, but not beyond that." "I will not get up in the middle of the night and make you a sandwich." "I won't take your drunken calls in the middle of the night."

Privacy didn't exist in my family. Simple things like saying those things are private, instead of hiding my poems or writing, where no one could find them, were not a given. As an adult I had to learn that it is okay to say this far but no farther. Like any new skill, I was not good at it initially and overreacted, pushing back harder than needed when I dealt with someone who cared about me. I had to learn to be patient with myself, and trust I would get better at it.

It took time to learn to say, I am not comfortable with that, instead of back the fuck off.

It Stops with Me

At some point in learning about family dysfunction, I realized that dysfunctions and issues tend to be passed down from generation to generation. We take those bad habits with us from one relationship to another, repeating the same mistakes, then wonder why things never improve. It was a conscious decision to say to myself, "It stops with me and it stops now." Sure, I had suffered the hurt and disappointments of living in that environment, but that didn't mean I had to continue it, and pass it on in my relationships and life.

Anger

One result of living in an environment where you don't matter and seeing some of the things I witnessed is rage. You can't come out of a world where you feel powerless to stop some horrible things around you without harboring a great deal of anger with no idea where to direct it. It often got pointed inwardly or taken out on those around me who had nothing to do with the cause. I found that using the method I described above of stopping when I felt myself about to go off, then excusing myself and separating the voices helped me diffuse a lot of anger. As I was going through my divorce, my father's voice was constantly repeating in my head, telling me that divorce was inevitable because I was ugly, stupid, and unlovable, so how could anyone possibly want to stay with me? There were times when I wanted to lash out at my ex. But separating the crap out of the past from the present situation allowed me to reduce my anger at myself significantly and her once I learned about cognitive behavioral therapy.

Attraction to Dysfunction

The old adage is "like attracts like" applies to you as you try to make your way in the world. There is a tendency to surround yourself with people who come from similar backgrounds, for both friends and lovers. Unfortunately, this often results in being surrounded by people who are unhealthy, or taking on projects. I sometimes found myself around people who are always negative, or who would try to take advantage of my willingness to give. It is justified internally by assuming you don't deserve better. I had to learn to surround myself with positive people, who treated me as an equal or a partner. I needed to learn to listen to that little voice inside that tries to warn me when something doesn't feel right. Relationships don't have to be hard or full of drama all the time, or a constant battle. Walk away from negative people because you don't need that in your life. Drama queens become addicted to the drama.

The other side of this, is that when things are going really well, don't sit waiting for the other shoe to drop. I found myself expecting a big blow up, or for this new fun person to leave because they see the real you. I had to learn to trust that I was worth the love they offered, get rid of those voices in my head that say different. That person sees more of you than think, and since they are still around you must be pretty great. Embrace the positive.

Chapter 59
Taking the Power Back

I learned small tips along the way from various sources that helped me. One thing that helped me a lot is that other people don't control your emotions. I can't remember exactly when I learned it in my studies of psychology. I used to say, "He makes me so mad." It didn't matter who it was, perhaps my brother for teasing me, or my father for continuing to drink. You give them the power to control your emotions with such thoughts.

Once, they explained to me how people out in the world act, and then you decide how you will react. The example that helped me was if your best friend called you an idiot, and you laugh and think, yeah, in this case, I did kind of act like one. If my father called me an idiot, or a teacher in front of my classmates, I would be pissed. Part of it is the situation, but it is still in your control. If you think, "I don't care what you think because I believe you are the idiot," you may just laugh at the teacher and walk away. The power to control your reactions is yours. Don't ever give it away.

Suppose there is someone you care about who does call you an idiot. Your best approach is not to call them an idiot also, but in a nonjudgmental way, explain to them how it makes you feel instead of striking back. If they don't apologize, you may want to re-evaluate your relationship.

New voices

Once I eliminated those old, abusive voices by identifying them and forming logical points to dispute them, I was amazed at the positive voices I found waiting for me. When I realized that now my mistakes cause me to laugh and call myself silly, versus stupid and idiot, it was a turning point in my emotional health. Find those gentle voices of encouragement in your life. They exist, and you can choose to listen to them.

Letting Go

As I said, much of the past can be a burden. The anger, the pain, and the secrets all get stuffed inside you and you carry them around. When you do that you give yourself no say in them continuing, no voice to make them stop. But once you confront them you gain independence. You can't let the past define you, the voices haunt you, or the burdens weigh you down. The only way they will serve you is to learn from them. You may have to unpack, evaluate, and set aside those that will not help you in your life. Do not carry them with you; the final step is to lay them down. Mentally toss them over the embankment, so no one else trips on them. You don't need them in your journey through life, and you will be lighter and happier without them.

So those issues that you see in this story, were mine. But no more. I posted them here so that others may learn to avoid or learn from them. They are no longer part of me. I have moved on. Nor should they be part of you. Leave them here.

As you pass through life with all its negative voices throwing seeds of doubt, self-loathing and hatred, may you learn to be an infertile ground and your garden will be full of the fruits and flowers you have planted on your journey.

Afterword

Dear Reader:

Thank you. If you enjoyed Infertile Ground, would you please write an honest review? Even if it is just a sentence or two. You have no idea how much it means to get a new review. You will also help all the people out there who use reviews to make decisions. Thank you so much.

If you are interested in learning about my novels and poetry, sign up for my guaranteed SPAM-free mailing list.

https://mailchi.mp/870edbe6ec1c/michaelpattonwritessignup

You can follow more frequent information and news about the author on his blog here:

https://michaelpatton.blog

Afterword

Or, if you would like to send me a note directly, use the following email address.

michael.patton.writes@gmail.com

Let me know what you think, and I'll also let you know when my next book is available.

About the Author

Michael L Patton has been writing poetry and short stories since he was in the third grade. He has had several articles published about his motorcycle adventures and been included in a regional anthology of poetry and stories. Michael enjoys exploring the complex relationships between family, friends and their pets. He has written four mystery/thriller novels in the Dan Williams and Syd Series, and published a book of poetry. He lives in northern California with his wife and his best friend Cyrus, their cat.

Made in United States
Troutdale, OR
08/12/2023